Praise for *In the Middle of the Mess*

"This book will not only change your life—it may just literally save your life. It is one rare, luminous, astonishingly brave book, saying what too many of us in the shadows have been desperate for someone to speak out loud for years. Sheila Walsh is not only a brazenly vulnerable, fearless warrior, she speaks unwavering truth that shatters the dark into a freeing light. It's a long time since I've read such a book and I weep for joy that someone finally wrote a literal lifeline. This woman is my hero."

—Ann Voskamp, *New York Times* bestselling author
of *The Broken Way* and *One Thousand Gifts*

"In this daring and breathtaking book, Sheila Walsh will take you by the hand and bring you to a place where it's okay not to be okay—a safe place of authenticity and hope where true healing abides. Don't hesitate. Let her guide you on this courageous journey of personal and spiritual discovery."

—Lee Strobel, *New York Times* bestselling
author of *The Case for Christ*

"*In the Middle of the Mess* boldly combats the lie that we are alone in our struggles and unqualified by them. In a world overrun by social media it's easy to forget that no one is without hardship. Sheila's beautiful vulnerability will remind us all that while we may see ourselves through the skewed filter of the world, God sees us through the cleansing blood of Jesus, perfect and whole."

—Lisa Bevere, *New York Times* bestselling
author of *Without Rival*

In the Middle
of the Mess

ALSO BY SHEILA WALSH

NONFICTION

The Longing in Me

Loved Back to Life

The Storm Inside

God Loves Broken People

The Shelter of God's Promises

Beautiful Things Happen

When a Woman Trusts God

Get Off Your Knees and Pray

God Has a Dream for Your Life

Let Go

All That Really Matters

Extraordinary Faith

I'm Not Wonder Woman but

God Made Me Wonderful

A Love So Big

Living Fearlessly

Stones from the River of Mercy

The Heartache No One Sees

Life Is Tough but God Is Faithful

Gifts for Your Soul

Honestly

Bring Back the Joy

The Best Devotions of Sheila Walsh

Sparks in the Dark

FICTION

Angel Song (with
Kathryn Cushman)

Sweet Sanctuary (with
Cindy Martinsen)

Song of the Brokenhearted
(with Cindy Martinsen)

CHILDREN'S BOOKS

Hello, Sun!

Hello, Stars!

God's Little Princess series

God's Mighty Warrior series

The Gnoo Zoo series

GIFT BOOKS

God's Shelter in Your Storm

Outrageous Love

Come As You Are

Good Morning, Lord

BIBLE STUDY CURRICULUM

The Longing in Me

The Storm Inside

The Shelter of God's Promises

COAUTHORED WOMEN OF FAITH BOOKS

Women of Faith Devotional Bible

Discovering God's Will for Your Life

The Great Adventure

Irrepressible Hope

Sensational Life

Time to Rejoice

Nothing Is Impossible

A Grand New Day

Infinite Grace

Contagious Joy

Laugh Out Loud

Amazing Freedom

*The Women of Faith
Daily Devotional*

The Women of Faith
Study Guide Series

In the Middle
of the Mess

STRENGTH FOR THIS
BEAUTIFUL, BROKEN LIFE

Sheila Walsh

NELSON
BOOKS
An Imprint of Thomas Nelson

Published in Nashville, Tennessee, by Nelson Books, an imprint of Thomas Nelson. Nelson Books and Thomas Nelson are registered trademarks of HarperCollins Christian Publishing, Inc.

Author is represented by the literary agency of Alive Communications, Inc., 7680 Goddard Street, Suite 200, Colorado Springs, CO 80920, www.alivecommunications.com.

Thomas Nelson titles may be purchased in bulk for educational, business, fund-raising, or sales promotional use. For information, please e-mail SpecialMarkets@ThomasNelson.com.

Unless otherwise noted, Scripture quotations are taken from the *Holy Bible*, New Living Translation. © 1996, 2004, 2007, 2013 by Tyndale House Foundation. Used by permission of Tyndale House Publishers, Inc., Carol Stream, Illinois 60188. All rights reserved.

Scriptures marked ESV are taken from the ESV® Bible (The Holy Bible, English Standard Version®), copyright © 2001 by Crossway, a publishing ministry of Good News Publishers. Used by permission. All rights reserved.

Scriptures marked NIV are taken from the Holy Bible, New International Version®, NIV®. Copyright © 1973, 1978, 1984, 2011 by Biblica, Inc.™ Used by permission of Zondervan. All rights reserved worldwide. www.zondervan.com. The "NIV" and "New International Version" are trademarks registered in the United States Patent and Trademark Office by Biblica, Inc.™

Scriptures marked AMP are taken from the Amplified® Bible, copyright © 1954, 1958, 1962, 1964, 1965, 1987 by The Lockman Foundation. Used by permission. (www.Lockman.org)

Scriptures marked HCSB are taken from the Holman Christian Standard Bible®, copyright © 1999, 2000, 2002, 2003, 2009 by Holman Bible Publishers. Used by permission. HCSB® is a federally registered trademark of Holman Bible Publishers.

Scriptures marked NKJV are taken from the New King James Version®. © 1982 by Thomas Nelson. Used by permission. All rights reserved.

Any Internet addresses, phone numbers, or company or product information printed in this book are offered as a resource and are not intended in any way to be or to imply an endorsement by Thomas Nelson, nor does Thomas Nelson vouch for the existence, content, or services of these sites, phone numbers, companies, or products beyond the life of this book.

ISBN 978-1-400204922 (eBook)
ISBN 978-1-400201853 (IE)

Library of Congress Cataloging-in-Publication Data

Names: Walsh, Sheila, 1956- author.
Title: In the middle of the mess : strength for this beautiful, broken life / Sheila Walsh.
Description: Nashville : Thomas Nelson, 2017. | Includes bibliographical references.
Identifiers: LCCN 2017006173 | ISBN 9781400204915
Subjects: LCSH: Spiritual life--Christianity. | Christian life. | Christian women--Religious life. | Grief--Religious aspects--Christianity.
Classification: LCC BV4501.3 .W361263 2017 | DDC 248.4--dc23 LC record available at https://lccn.loc.gov/2017006173

Printed in the United States of America

17 18 19 20 21   LSC   10 9 8 7 6 5 4 3 2 1

This book is dedicated with love and gratitude to every brave soul who chooses life day after day in the middle of the mess. You are beautiful to me.

"Once you are real you can't become unreal again. It lasts for always."

—Margery Williams

Contents

✧

Foreword

When my friend Sheila Walsh told me her next book would chronicle her lifelong struggle with suicidal thoughts, I cried. I cried for her—for the terrible suffering she has endured with the dark thoughts that accompany major depression. I cried for my son, Matthew, who lost his courageous fight with mental illness. But I also cried tears of relief for the women who will read this book and find unbelievable comfort, strength, and HOPE as they recognize—maybe for the first time—that their immense pain is understood, shared, and validated, not only by Sheila, but by a loving Father. If you've ever told yourself "this world would be better off without me" or "I can't do this another day," please read *In the Middle of the Mess*. You'll find a sister who gets you, who is walking the same road you are, and who is learning how to survive and even thrive (*OR live*) in the middle of the mess of this broken and beautiful life.

Kay Warren, cofounder of Saddleback Church

Introduction

I have a black-and-white photo of my father on my desk. He's smiling, face turned upward to the sun. He's clearly posing for my mum, looking very Rudolph Valentino. Sometimes I talk to him. I know it's a strange confession, but I don't suppose I've been one to shy away from confession. When I talk to him, I tell him I wish things could have turned out differently. I wish I could have shared the truths I've learned, the truths of this book. Maybe it would have saved his life.

He's been gone so many years now, but even still, I'm dedicating this book to him. If I could see him today—just one last time—if I could slip him these pages and a letter, I think I'd tell him the whole truth, and here's what that letter might say.

Dear Dad,

Most days I'm okay, but the messy days, and then the even darker days, still scare me. You knew this feeling. Didn't you?

I used to have a nightmare after you died. I was falling down a deep, dark hole, and no one could hear me crying for help. Only five years old, I'd wake in the middle of the night in a panic, sweat pouring down my back and face, my Deputy Dawg pajamas soaked through. I didn't want to wake anyone, so I'd just open the toy closet and climb in. I'd stay there until the morning, holding Big Billy, my bear, until I fell asleep. I never told anyone.

It was strange how Mum and the rest of the family never talked about how you died. I tried to broach the topic once when I was about eight years old. We were sitting around the kitchen table, and when I said how sad she must be when she thinks about you, she left the table and went upstairs. If I hadn't felt so responsible for how you died, I'd have forced that conversation open. But I couldn't bring myself to do it, just as I couldn't force myself out of the toy closet where I felt safe from my nightmares.

After your funeral, Mum took all your pictures down and put them away in a safe place—a small, locked suitcase under her bed. Memories of you were mostly off-limits. We moved back to her hometown, distanced ourselves from your memory. She cried sometimes but always behind closed doors. We had to grieve and question in our own ways. I think we were all lonely. I know I was.

When I was ten years old, I came home early from school one day when I wasn't feeling well. Mum tucked me in bed, and after she brought me a cup of tea, she sat on the edge of the bed beside me. Since we were alone, I asked her how you died.

She said that you fell into the river. She said the coroner wrote "death by drowning." She'd said it as if you'd lost your way in the dark and stumbled into the water. I think part of what she believed was true. You did lose your way in the dark, didn't you? But it wasn't the moonless-country dark of Ayrshire. It was the dark inside you that made life unbearable, wasn't it?

You were so young—only thirty-four—and you were trapped inside a body that had turned against you. Your mind didn't even have the decency to endure the dark, to stay secreted away in it. In those moments when the red clouds inside your brain cleared, you saw your future, the shape of it, and it wasn't pretty. I don't know that for certain, but somehow, I believe it's true.

I know Mum visited you after you went to live in that place, but I never got to come. I wish I had. Perhaps if you saw that I could handle your shadow side, you might have been able to hold on a bit longer. I don't know. I just wish I could have told you that I still loved you, that I always had and always would.

I'd like you to know the truth: People don't understand that what children imagine is so much worse than what's true. Now I know. You were broken. Just like me. I know there were days when you were my dad and other days when you became that scary monster lashing out, raging inside and out, lost, alone. The last time you ever looked at me, you weren't yourself and you must have seen how terrified I was. The look in your eyes stayed with me for years, and I wondered if the look in mine pushed you over the edge. But now I understand that's not true: I know your death wasn't my fault.

I live with dark despair too. I have seen how it takes over. And knowing that aching loneliness, knowing the ways it haunts, I wish I could go back and hold your hand. I wish I could fight it with you, wish I could smile at you one last time. Just one. Maybe that would have given you the strength to hold on a little longer.

When I was fifteen, a woman in our church was talking to my best friend about the place where you died. Perhaps she'd forgotten that you had been there. She worked there and said the place was a "house of horrors"—not a place for children. She smelled of mothballs and Youth Dew. The Ayrshire Lunatic Asylum, she said, and I couldn't help but wonder: *Asylum? Isn't that supposed to be a safe place with safe rooms? Don't people leave their war-torn countries and beg for asylum in countries where they know they'll be protected? Why couldn't they protect you?* And now, I'm left with only questions, unanswered.

When you escaped that night, did you have a plan?

Did you know where you were going, or did you just want to get away?

Were you trying to find your way home?

In my adult years I willed myself to visit that river. Shadows and silence had nearly killed me. They had dropped me into a place similar to one where you'd last lived. But I couldn't bring myself to do it until I was thirty-six years old; that's when the compulsion to see the water finally became too great. I had to go. I wanted to understand.

When you last saw me, I was five, but I'm now sixty. Mum died last month, and I find myself adrift. I have a caring husband and a darling son, and I'm on the best medication out there, but there are days when it's not enough. Some days I feel as if I live on the edge of a razor and could fall off at any moment. It's hard to say that out loud, because I know how this works: People will want to fix me. The truth is, I don't think "fixed" is what I'm looking for. What I want is what I wish we'd been able to do a long time ago—to tell the truth, first to God, and then among friends, in a community of understanding, for as long as it takes to heal. I wish you could have done this too.

I'm not afraid of pain; I'm afraid of the silence that leaves us all alone. I'm afraid of the secrets that left you all alone. Amid the silence and secrets, it's easy to believe every desperate lie inside our heads, every monster that hunts us. I know you understand that. So, for my sake and in your memory, I'm going to speak up. I'm hoping, I'm praying, that it might give another person the space and the grace to see that it's okay not to be okay. I want to show others how to find strength in the middle of the mess. I think knowing how to do that is a gift, a beautiful miracle straight from God.

So I'm punching a hole in the silence. I'm kicking in the

door of secrets that keeps us cold and lonely. We need a place to show up in our brokenness and still be loved, a safe place where we can come as we are. I'm committed to that now, for myself and everyone who hurts. It's time to tell the truth. We don't have to hide anymore.

I used to believe that I was alone in the darkness. I never was. On the days when I couldn't hold on by myself, Jesus held on to me. I see it now. He always was my safe place. Now, when I feel as if I'm falling, I hold on to Him, and I wish you could have learned to hold on that way. I know, in eternity, that you have.

> I love you always,
> Sheila

It's okay not to be okay.

On the *days*

when I couldn't

hold on by

myself,

Jesus held

on to *me.*

Chapter 1

❦

Everyday Salvation

*First there is the fall, and then we recover
from the fall. Both are the mercy of God.*

—JULIAN OF NORWICH

Every morning the sun comes up anyway.

—RICH MULLINS

I looked at my face in my dressing room mirror—pale and tired. I was losing weight. I wasn't trying to, but I didn't have the heart to eat these days. I felt sick and cold inside. What was wrong with me?

It was time for my daily television show, and Gail, our floor director, entered my room. "Five minutes to air," she said. I picked up my notes, headed out into the studio, and took my seat on the set of *Heart to Heart with Sheila Walsh*.

The lights came up, and the heat set against my cheeks. The director pointed to me, and I opened.

"Hello, and welcome. I'm sure you've heard other recording artists perform songs such as 'Sing Your Praise to the Lord' and

1

'Awesome God.' Today's guest has written these and other hit songs. But not only is he a writer and recording artist, he also feels a responsibility to be real, to tell the truth, to be genuine with his audiences. His latest album, *The World As Best As I Remember It, Volume 2*, gives us a hint: he spends time thinking about life. Welcome, Rich Mullins."

The studio audience offered conservative church applause, and the cameras turned to Rich at the piano as he sang, "Oh God, You are my God, and I will ever praise You." There was something about the way he sang, the depth of his lyrics, and the pain that welled into that chorus; it was as if that aching was just beneath the surface, haunting his music. It was both a comforting and unsettling piece, the kind of song that leaves you feeling raw and ragged. The lyrics bored down to the place where my secret lived, a secret I could never tell.

After playing his opening number, Rich walked from the piano and took a seat opposite me on the studio set. The applause died down, and I asked Rich my first question. "What are the most important things in your life?"

I still remember his answer.

"At any given moment it might be slightly different, but I would imagine that nothing would be more important than becoming fully who you were supposed to be. You know what I mean? For me, that's what salvation is all about."

I wish I'd known how profound his response was. I wish I'd dug deeper and asked him to talk more about his understanding of salvation, the process of becoming more fully who we're supposed to be. I had no idea how much I would need his wisdom in the weeks and years ahead—the wisdom of a thirty-six-year-old musician. Instead, I pushed forward with my preplanned questions.

"How are you different at thirty-six than twenty-six?"

"Oh, I'm very different," he said. "I have failed enough that I've learned that it's not the end of the world to make mistakes . . . every morning the sun comes up anyway. I think when you stop being afraid of failing, you become a lot more free."

Throughout the interview, Rich talked about accountability, community, and the loneliness of not being known. He was speaking to my deepest pains, my deepest needs, but I didn't quite understand yet. What's more, I didn't know how to ask for help. The very idea of being free, of being fully who God created me to be, felt cruel and unattainable.

I didn't know God had a plan in place to help me understand. I didn't know that in just a few weeks everything in my life would come crashing down and this would be the beginning of a fresh understanding of salvation for me. I didn't know that this kind of salvation—the salvation Rich spoke of—isn't a pretty process. Sometimes it's a costly, bloody mess.

I hadn't thought about this interview with Rich Mullins in years, but his name kept coming up in conversations. So I decided to find the interview on YouTube. When I did, I asked my husband, Barry, if he wanted to watch it with me. The familiar music began, and as the show opened, I was transported back to that time and place.

Neither of us said anything for a few moments. Then Barry asked, "Do you see the date of this show?"

"Yes. It's May 1992," I said. Then I realized the significance of the date.

"How long was it before you ended up in the psych hospital?"

"Three months."

"But you look fine. If I didn't know, I'd never believe you were on the edge of a breakdown."

I didn't know whether to laugh or cry. He was right. I looked very put together and in control, but I was dying inside, disappearing a little more every day.

"I was very good at looking fine. That was one of my problems."

"It's not only that. Listen to your accent," Barry said. "I've watched some shows you taped in 1990. But here, you sound so much more Scottish. I wonder why?"

I thought for a moment, remembering those dark days. "I think I was falling down a hole back to where it all began," I said.

My interview with Rich was only weeks before my collapse, but I looked fine.

Day after day, I sat with a studio audience and told them that God loved them and everything would turn out well. And I believed this with all my heart—at least for the audience members. But I was utterly convinced that I was too far away, too lost inside myself for the good news to reach my every pain. There were broken places I'd hidden from light so I didn't have to feel the pain quite so much, but those places were pushed deep into my soul, far away from healing too.

Perhaps I hid the pain because it was in the past, and I knew one day I'd be home with Christ and all my struggles would be gone. I just had to hang on until then. I believed the past was taken care of and the future was secure. But I didn't know how to live fully saved, fully myself, fully in the present. I didn't understand what Rich meant when he said salvation is found in becoming fully who you are supposed to be—*right now, in the present.*

I wonder how many people live the same way. How many of our friends? Our family members? Our fellow churchgoers? I wonder how many pastors step into their pulpits on Sunday mornings bringing words of life and hope to others while they keep their pain secretly hidden?

Frederick Buechner paints a picture of it: "The preacher pulls the little cord that turns on the lectern light and deals out his note cards like a riverboat gambler. The stakes have never been higher. Two minutes from now he may have lost his listeners completely to their own thoughts, but at this minute he has them in the palm of his hand."[1]

Will he tell the truth? Will he let us into his mess? It's a hard thing to do when everyone looks to you for help. The temptation to say *the right thing* is almost insufferable.

God is good.
God loves you.
He is powerful and He is on the throne.
His strength is made perfect in your weakness.

You can hear these words booming from the pulpit, can't you?

The trouble is—and this was true of me all those years ago—many of us already know *the right thing* to say, and we let it roll off our tongues without hesitation. But if we were to stop and ponder, we might find that what is intended to be a helpful reminder can also be a dangerous prison. It can also make us feel that there's something wrong with us.

I wonder how many of my churchgoing friends believe that sharing the broken truth about their lives would alienate them from church? Are they asking, "If God is good, why do I still feel so bad inside? If God loves me, why do I feel so alone, so unloved?"

For years, I appeared on television or stood onstage and talked about the love and mercy of God. What I didn't understand was just how wide and deep that mercy is. I didn't understand that I still needed saving—from the secrets, lies, and pain that haunted me.

My internal pain is difficult to speak aloud because it's so unspeakably complicated. There's no easy way to sugarcoat this. I've been tormented by thoughts of suicide for most of my life—first of my father's, then of my own. Is this a shocking confession? It is to most people, and it should be. But when someone you love takes their life, when suicide moves from the realm of the unthinkable to part of your family story, the demons of that reality come calling.

When I was very young I didn't think about ending my life. As a child it was different. I had a recurring nightmare—I was about to be executed for a crime I hadn't committed. I was led down a long corridor to an execution chamber, which was stone on one side and glass on the other. I could see my family through the glass, but they couldn't see me. They were talking and laughing and couldn't hear my screams for help. I woke up each night, sweating and heart pounding, just as I reached the chamber. I'd crawl out of bed and hide in the toy closet covered in my soft toys until the morning. I never told anyone. It was my shameful little secret.

The dreams haunted and haunted, and when I was nineteen, it all became too much. I was a student at London Theological Seminary, training to become a missionary in India. I didn't realize it then, but I had convinced myself that if I became a missionary—if I did something I didn't really want to do but did it for God—then God would see how much I loved Him. Maybe He'd take away the pain, the torment, the nightmares. But no matter what I did, or how hard I tried, it never felt like enough. The pain and fear never passed. I came to believe that I would never balance the scales; I'd never be able to pay for what I'd done to my family. The nightmares would never stop. And so, I took a train into the heart of London on a dreary English evening. I walked around in the rain for a while until I was soaked to the skin.

My life didn't make sense to me. I loved God and I believed He loved me, but I felt lost and sad. After hours, I hustled to the station to catch the last train, and that's when it happened. I walked to the bridge over the railway tracks and looked down. The voices came: *Jump! Just jump. It'll be over in a moment.*

The voices called, but I woke up to the terrifying darkness of it all. I mustered my courage and called out the only name that I knew would help: *"Jesus!"* The voices stopped, and I stepped away from the edge, from the execution chamber, and back onto the safety of the bridge. Heart pounding, tears rolling down my face, I felt ashamed and frightened. It was the first time I remember the feeling that would become so commonplace in my adult years. I was afraid of myself.

This would be an easier story to tell if it had only happened once, but it didn't. Some nights, I've looked at a bottle of pills and thought how easy it would be to swallow the whole lot. I had other thoughts of jumping, of slitting my wrists.

Thirty years after that night on the bridge those suicidal thoughts remained. Sometimes it would be a fleeting thought, but there was one night when I knew that I was in a battle for my life. I don't remember much about that day, but as evening fell I felt such a weight of darkness on my soul. Fifteen years earlier I had been diagnosed with clinical depression, but that night I began to understand the hellish dance between depression and spiritual warfare.

Christian had fallen fast asleep. Barry could tell I wasn't doing well and suggested I take a bath and relax. I couldn't. I told him I was fine and just needed a little alone time. As the night wore on, the house grew cold and still, and it felt as if evil had crawled through cracks in the wall. The evil seeped across the floorboards and down to my toes. It crept up my shins, up my torso, up my neck. It stuck to me.

The weapon that night was a large knife. I saw it lying on the draining board in the kitchen, and the voices were deafening.

Just pick it up. It won't hurt. It will be over soon. You don't have to live like this anymore.

I walked into the living room and lay facedown on the carpet. All I could say over and over was one name: *"Jesus! Jesus! Jesus!"*

The hours passed—one o'clock, two o'clock. At three in the morning something inside me shifted. I remembered whose I was. I stood up and shouted out, "No!" I picked up a verse I've known since I was a child and wielded it like a weapon, "For everyone who calls on the name of the Lord will be saved" (Rom. 10:13 HCSB).

I called that verse out loud and I believed it. I called on His name and believed Him. I had been saved from hell and into eternity ever since, as an eleven-year-old girl, I accepted Jesus as my Savior. But that night I needed saving in the present, and I knew it. It wasn't that I needed to become a Christian again; instead, I needed the power of the living Word of God to save me from the present tormentors. And that night, as I called on the name of the Lord, I found Him pushing back the darkness, the evil—all those suicidal thoughts. I felt Him saving me.

This is the truth I would discover that night: Christ came to save us in this present moment. The gift of salvation is God's active, present gift to us, no matter where we are.

That was the night I truly grasped the truth of Ephesians 6:12. My battle was "not against flesh and blood, but against the rulers, against the authorities, against the powers of this dark world and against the spiritual forces of evil in the heavenly realms" (NIV). And this battle was one for my life.

It's the same in your life, too, isn't it? Even if you aren't plagued by depression or thoughts of suicide, you have your own struggles, big and small. Perhaps you're a single mom at the end of your rope. You feel all alone, and at times you take your frustration out on the ones you love the most.

Maybe you just can't get your head above water financially, and every day feels like a struggle to make ends meet.

Perhaps your own body has betrayed you. Chronic sickness is debilitating not only to the body but also to the soul.

Or perhaps you work with people who make life difficult. No matter what you try to make things better, they seem committed to making your life hard.

Sometimes it's the great, big darkness that swallows us whole. But often, it's the small, daily things that wear us down the most. How can we be saved from the very things that are woven into the tapestry of our daily lives?

Too often the meaning of salvation is reduced to a simplistic formula. The very question "Are you saved?" implies a once-and-for-all action. In terms of receiving Christ as Savior, asking to be forgiven for our sins, it's certainly that. And that would be all we'd need if the presence of sin was gone the moment we became Christians. You just tick the box and move on. If all our brokenness was healed the moment we came to Christ, we'd have no need to call on His name over and over again—but that's not my story, and I suspect it's not yours either.

My friend Nicky Gumbel, vicar of Holy Trinity Church in London, wrote, "'Salvation' . . . is a huge and comprehensive word. It means 'freedom' . . . There are three tenses of salvation: we have been set free from the penalty of sin, we are being set free from the power of sin and we will be set free from the presence of sin."[2]

So, when you confess your sin to Christ, your past is gone—the penalty paid in full. And in this confession, we also know that Christ secures our glorious, eternal future. This eternal future is one free of sin, grief, and pain. As John wrote in the book of Revelation, "God Himself will be with them and be their God. He will wipe away every tear from their eyes. Death will no longer exist; grief, crying, and pain will exist no longer, because the previous things have passed away" (21:3–4 HCSB).

But that's not it; there's more.

There is a present-tense salvation, one that's offered to us right now in the middle of our mess. Salvation is far greater and more present than we imagine. The Greek word for is *sózó*. It means "to save, to deliver, to heal, and to make whole." And that delivering, that healing, is a daily and ongoing process.

Christ can save us from the present experience of pain and shame, no matter how ugly the internal terrain is. To me, my present pain is unspeakably ugly, and it's been that way since long before the night in the London train station. I've kept secrets for so long—still do from time to time. I've nursed shame the way a child nurses a blanket. In those days, I didn't know how desperately I needed Christ's ongoing salvation. I didn't even know it was available, but as I look back over my life, Jesus was standing with outstretched arms offering it in so many ways: through the Word, His church, and a ragamuffin musician like Rich Mullins. He wanted to free me to be who I was created to be—one who didn't struggle with secrets and shame.

Do you want that kind of freedom? Freedom to be who you were meant to be apart from your own pain and shame, big or small?

You might wonder whether this kind of salvation is possible for you. Can we live in this world without fear of failing and without the shame attached to it? I think it depends on how you define *failing*.

A friend called and told me that she struggles with online pornography. Isn't that something only men struggle with? She told me she'd reached out to her small group the previous year, and very gingerly she'd begun the discussion by saying that perhaps women can wrestle with this temptation too. She took the first step, tried to invite others into her process of daily, present salvation. But the looks of disgust in the eyes of the other women in her group shut her down. That's when it set in—one more year of lonely hell, shame, and bitter condemnation.

She took a risk calling me. I'm grateful for her courage. I told her that her struggle was no different from mine or the self-righteous women who shut her down. I think we fear what we don't understand. We did some research together and found a group of women in her area who understand this dark wrestling match with pornography. Community is saving her. She's not alone.

I have a girlfriend who's an alcoholic. She's in treatment for the second time. If she could move to a world where no alcohol existed, then perhaps she could stop being so afraid of failing again. Once she said these words to me on the phone: "I'm a failure. I'm a horrible person." I understood why she felt that way. She's a mom. Her children have seen her drunk, and her struggles have impacted her family. But though she fell and it wasn't pretty, she didn't stop there. Instead, she resolved to get back up, and she's trying again. She's wrestling with the beast that wants to steal her days by offering what she craves.

I wasn't allowed to call her during her six weeks of inpatient treatment. I could write to her and pray for her. Daily I asked Jesus to be present with her through others who understand her struggle, through His Word, and through quiet prayer. She called me when she was on her way home to her family—shaky, vulnerable, but tasting hope. Her greatest fear, she said, would be to fall again after believing she was healed. I told her I believe it's possible to be healed and to fall again and again. Grace doesn't come with a sell-by date, I said.

---

*I believe it's possible to be healed
and to fall again and again. Grace
doesn't come with a sell-by date.*

I reminded her of Paul's promise: "And I am certain that God, who began the good work within you, will continue his work until it is finally finished on the day when Christ Jesus returns" (Phil. 1:6).

If we are still on this earth, then the work is not finished. God has committed to work with us in that journey until Christ returns. How I wish for a greater understanding of this in the body of Christ. Too often we judge, measure, condemn, and isolate. The gospel of Jesus Christ invites us to sit together in our rags under the wide-open sky of grace. Does that mean it doesn't matter how we live? No. What I mean is that condemnation and isolation are the tools of the enemy. The Holy Spirit brings conviction, which draws us closer to Christ. Condemnation pushes us back into the darkness.

We all have struggles, though they look different—booze, anger, bitterness, pills, disconnection from our children or spouse, drugs, discontent with our career, conflict with our boss or neighbor, porn, depression, physical illness—it's all the stuff of present brokenness.

And though we, the church, have little grace for certain struggles, that is why Jesus came. He came to save us for eternity, yes, but He also came to save us today.

I remember the morning I picked up my local newspaper and read the headline that had my name in it. I'd had a nervous breakdown on national television, just weeks after the Rich Mullins interview. I was so ashamed. Lying on my bedroom carpet, curled up in a fetal position, I cried until I had no tears left. I prayed over and over, "I'm sorry. I'm sorry. I'm so sorry that I've let You down." Although I've never heard God's audible voice, I perceived—in the deepest broken part of me—God saying, "My child, do you believe that I love you?"

That was the most important question of all, the one that's redefined me. It has never been about me getting it right. You either. We've got it all upside down. We see from the earth up, but God sees from heaven down. We see ourselves from the perspective of the mud we're sitting in, but God sees us through the blood of Christ that washes us clean, in the present, in the middle of our messes. And in His love, He wants to save us—in the present. He wants to give us strength for our broken, beautiful lives.

You don't have to pretend to like where you are right now. In fact, God already knows where you are. As Psalm 44:21 says, God knows the secrets of our hearts. If you trust that the Father loves you, then you can tell the whole truth.

Even Jesus spoke to God about the hard things of His present life on earth. In the Garden that night, praying in agony so intense He thought He might die, He asked God to deliver Him from His pain, His torment. "Take this cup from me," He said. But Christ finished His prayer by saying, "Yet not my will, but yours be done" (Luke 22:42 NIV). Jesus showed us what to do when we are stuck. He told the truth but said to His Father: I trust You with the outcome.

We can tell God what's true. He knows that the things we

We see ourselves from the perspective of the mud we're sitting in, but God sees us through the blood of Christ that washes us clean, in the present, in the middle of our messes.

hide—the things we are afraid to talk about—control us in ways we don't even realize. But as followers of Christ's way, we get to say:

I hate this.
I'm scared.
I don't know what's going to happen next.
This is not what I wanted.
I'm so disappointed in myself.
Take this cup from me.

We don't need to pretend. We can say what's true, praying for Christ to come and save us—in any moment, amid any circumstance. And this might be the most honest worship you've ever offered in your whole life. You tell the truth and take the next step to being who God made you to be—a dearly loved daughter, saved from circumstance, saved from guilt and shame.

In his letter to the church in Thessalonica, Paul wrote: "But we behaved gently when we were among you, like a devoted mother tenderly caring for her own children. Having such a deep affection for you, we were delighted to share with you not only God's good news but also our own lives, because you had become so very dear to us" (1 Thess. 2:7–8 AMP).

He was clearly very fond of the people in Thessalonica. He was respected as one of the most influential leaders of the early church, and he left a pattern of vulnerability for us to follow. He opened his life to others. Yes, he shared the good news of the risen Christ, but he also walked beside other believers and shared his joys and sorrows, his struggles and hopes. I've always found it easier to simply share the good news, but true community demands both the Word and our lives. And that's my hope for this book: that you'll see how community has worked out in my life, and how it can work out in yours.

I don't know what you're struggling with right now, whether you're angry or crippled with self-loathing or sadness. Perhaps you have endured dark days in the past, or you will face dark days tomorrow, next week, or next year. But I know this: You are not alone. Even more, you are loved. You don't have to keep secrets or believe lies. There is a safe place where you can find healing. Would you like to find it?

This is the invitation of this book—an invitation to find healing, to find strength in the middle of your mess. But it's not just a book about vulnerability, about sharing (or oversharing). It's a book of practices. It's a book about confession, about letting go, about picking up the Word of God, which was fashioned for your own personal war with your own personal demons. This is a book intended to give you strength. This is the book I wish I could have read before my meltdown. This is the book I wish I could have read again just before my mother's passing.

⚬⚬

In my interview with Rich Mullins, he quoted his friend Brennan Manning. Rich said, "When [Brennan] gets home, he believes that perhaps Christ will look him in the face and say, 'Did you believe that I loved you? Did you really believe it?' Because if you believe that, it changes everything."

I considered this quote as I listened one more time to that interview with Rich. I realized that he was saying something that I didn't understand at the time. Salvation is about becoming who you were created to be—a well-loved daughter of God. I know that now.

I was born to be a well-loved little girl, free of secrets and self-hatred. You were made to be that, too, my darling friend. Do you believe it? Do you want to?

Reflection

Facing the whole truth about ourselves can be very hard, but I know now there is freedom in offering our broken, beautiful lives to Christ. He gave everything for us so that we could be saved. It's a holy offering to give everything back to Him.

What messes are you facing today? Have you shared them with God—including the ones you've tried to hide from yourself? Read the scripture below. What does it say to you about God's love in the midst of brokenness?

> For I received from the Lord that which I also delivered to you: that the Lord Jesus on the same night in which He was betrayed took bread; and when He had given thanks, He broke it and said, "Take, eat; this is My body which is broken for you; do this in remembrance of Me."
>
> —1 Corinthians 11:23–24 NKJV

Chapter 2

Burying Our Secrets

No one ever told me that grief felt so like fear.

—C. S. LEWIS, *A GRIEF OBSERVED*

T he buzzing noise woke me. At first I thought it was the alarm on my phone, waking me to start the day. I tried to punch the snooze button, but the buzz continued. I finally picked up the phone and looked at the screen. It was a call from Scotland, from my sister. I bolted upright, uneasy to be getting a call at such an early hour.

"Hi. Are you guys okay?" I asked.

She was silent, then I heard her take a deep breath.

"She's gone, Sheila."

I wrestled to clear my mind, to comprehend her words. I thought perhaps Mum had been admitted again. She had been struggling with Alzheimer's for the last few years and had fought a battle with bladder cancer. She'd been in and out of the hospital several times.

Frances remained silent, and as I let her words sink in, I woke into knowing. My mum had taken her final breath on this earth and her first breath in the presence of Christ.

"What happened?" I asked.

"It was very quick," Frances said. "She didn't feel well when she woke this morning, then she had a bit of a seizure. The doctor isn't sure if it was a stroke or a heart attack, but she was gone before the EMS team got there."

I forced my mind to process a response.

"I'll book the first flight I can get," I said. We exchanged good-byes and hung up.

I stared at the dark wall across the room. It felt surreal. I wanted to pick up the phone, dial Mum's number, and hear her voice one more time. She had been growing steadily weaker, but I had gifts to send for her upcoming eighty-eighth birthday. I just didn't expect to hear that she was gone.

There is something so primal about a mum. Even those who don't have great relationships with their mothers often grieve deeply when that one person who brought them into this world is gone. The previous Christmas, I'd had an overwhelming desire to see her face-to-face, so I made a spontaneous trip to Scotland.

Frances and her husband, Ian, picked me up at the Glasgow airport, and we drove to Mum's nursing home, Airlie House, a place for the senior members of the small church in Scotland where I grew up. My sister and I had moved Mum to Airlie several years before when it became clear that it wasn't safe for her to live alone. She'd become forgetful and frail, and we were afraid she'd fall when she was alone. We worried she'd forget to take her medication or lock the door at night. Airlie House was our solution, a place of community where others would watch over her 24/7.

When Frances's car pulled up to the grey, two-story stone house, I hardly waited for her to put it into park. I bolted out and proceeded to the front door to ring the bell. One of the staff let us in, and I bee-lined toward the communal lounge. I couldn't wait to see the look on Mum's face when she saw me. I found her sitting in a chair, and I knelt in front of her. Then with my arms thrown wide and a big grin on my face, I delivered a Broadway-worthy, "Ta-da!"

Mum looked at me, but she didn't respond. Then she turned to my sister.

Mum didn't know me.

"It's Sheila, Mum!" Frances exclaimed. "She's flown over to see you."

Mum stared at me for another moment then gave that sweet smile she made when being introduced to people for the first time.

Eventually, though, she recognized me.

"Sheila! It's so lovely to see you! How's the weather?"

I wasn't quite sure if she meant the weather in Dallas or outside of Airlie House.

"It's lovely," I said. "No rain so far."

"Good! Don't want you to get wet," she said with a soft smile. "How was school?" I'd graduated from Mainholm Academy in 1974. Now it was 2015. Had she lost the last forty-one years of our lives?

I cried a lot that night. I felt robbed, lonely.

Many years earlier, my dad's death had left Mum with three children to raise alone, but rather than trying to hold on tightly to my sister, brother, and me, she always encouraged us to follow our passions. I knew that it was hard for her when I moved to America, but she cheered me on, believing I was right where God wanted me to be. Mum and I had always been close, and we had remained that way, despite the miles.

During this visit, though, in many ways we were strangers. I wasn't sure which year of my story she was reliving. Did she remember that I was married, or did she imagine me single? Did she remember her nineteen-year-old grandson living in the States?

I would be in Scotland only four days, so I spent as much time as I could beside my mum. There were times she wanted to talk, and times we sat without exchanging a word. One morning she thanked me for my Christmas gifts.

"Did you like them?" I asked, going along with her even though I hadn't given her any gifts yet.

"I do," she said. "I love the car and the dog."

In her mind, I must have been extraordinarily generous yet misguided because Mum never learned to drive. I suppose her real memories were on shelves too high to reach.

The four days passed, and the time for me to fly back to America arrived. Mum said good-bye as if I were going to the corner store rather than across the ocean. I hugged her, not knowing it would be the last time this side of heaven.

Following my sister's early-morning phone call, I immediately began making preparations to go home to Scotland. I booked the same flight I'd taken the previous Christmas. From Dallas to Philadelphia, then on to Glasgow, Scotland. Ian picked me up at the airport and we drove the forty minutes to Ayr, the little seaside town where I was raised. Frances was waiting at her front door. As we hugged under the slate-grey sky, tears ran down our faces. We said the things you say when your mum passes into memory, into eternity.

"I'm so glad she didn't suffer."

"That's how she would have wanted to go."

"She lived her whole life with this moment in mind."

"She's home."

Everything we said was true, but all I could think was, *I wish I could talk to her just one more time.* I had a sickening, desperate feeling inside, as if I were trying to remember something important that was just beyond my reach.

"Let me make you a cup of tea," Ian said. "You and Frances have a lot to talk about."

I sank into the cream-leather sofa in their den, and Frances sat by the fire.

"Mum left a very detailed letter about her funeral service," she said.

"She did? When did she write it?" I asked.

"A long time ago," she said, passing the letter to me.

I had to smile. "Just like Mum, organized to the last breath."

She'd requested two hymns—"Loved with Everlasting Love" and "Through the Love of God, Our Savior"—even specifying the melodies they were to be sung to.

"What about notifying her friends?" I asked.

Frances picked up Mum's familiar red-leather address book.

"My fingers are numb!" she said. "I've called everyone in here."

I paused for a moment before asking, "Where is she now?"

"At Co-operative Funeralcare," she said. "They've been wonderful. They arranged for an announcement in the local newspaper, helped with flowers, and ordered cars for the family."

"I can't believe she's gone," I said, tears dripping into my teacup.

"I know. I can't either."

I wanted to say good-bye to Mum one last time before we buried her, so I made my way to the funeral parlor. I asked the funeral director for a few private moments. In the plain brown wooden casket, Mum looked as if she were sleeping, almost as if she could sit up at any moment and begin talking to me. I pulled back the satin sheet that covered most of her chest and noted her pretty pink suit, the suit Frances had chosen for her burial. Her hands were folded over her chest, left over right. And there it was. The thin, worn band of gold. Mum and Dad were married in 1953, and she hadn't taken off her wedding ring since the day she said "I do." It was a promise of marriage when she received it, but after my dad died, it became a promise that one day she would see him again.

I remembered the stories she'd told me of her childhood, how she could never please her father. No matter how good her grades were, he'd tell her they could have been better. I thought of the young woman who wanted to be a nurse but had to leave school at fifteen to help her mum raise three younger siblings as her dad's Alzheimer's set in. I remembered her glow when she told how she'd found the man of her dreams, how together they had three children. Then I considered how she lost that man—my dad—first to a brain aneurysm and then to suicide.

She'd suffered so much disappointment and pain, but she never talked about it. These were her secrets. I looked at the body, the now-empty shell that once housed all her hopes, dreams, and nightmares. I ached to know them better, but now I never would. These are the things death takes from us.

"I know this isn't easy," Frances said later that day, "but when you feel up to it, we need to clean out her room at Airlie."

"Let's do it now and get that bit over with," I said. We put on our raincoats, ran to her car, and headed out. Frances rang the bell and waited for one of the staff to let us in. We made our way down the long corridor to Mum's room, and the moment I opened the door, I began to sob. It was all there: the carefully made bed, her favorite armchair from home, her pink slippers, her Bible on the nightstand, her tithing envelope sitting ready for church. I looked at the pile of unread books and a half-eaten candy bar. Simple reminders that death gave Mum no warning bell. It was so familiar, but she wasn't there anymore.

The staff made it clear that we didn't have to hurry to clean out her stuff, but we knew that at Airlie, another family was already waiting for her room. I wiped my tears and Frances, Ian, and I got to work. We packed her clothes into suitcases, her books and CDs into boxes. We took the pictures and framed family photographs off the walls and wrapped them in newspaper for safekeeping. The final picture hung over her bed. One of Mum's dearest friends had embroidered it for her. Two words followed by an exclamation point: *Yes, Lord!*

Frances looked at me, eyes tender. "Would you like to have that?" she asked.

"I would," I said. I took it off the wall, wrapped it in a scarf I'd sent Mum a few Christmases ago, and put it in my backpack.

"Can I have this too?" I asked, holding up a stuffed rabbit.

"Why would you want that?" Frances asked.

"It was beside her pillow," I said. "She loved this silly rabbit. Perhaps she shared her secrets with him."

❧

In Scotland the family members lower the casket into the ground. My brother, sister, and I were at the head, Ian and my two nephews were at the foot, and Christian and Dominic—Mum's other grandsons—were in the middle. The rain bounced off the casket, off our overcoats and hats. We lowered it into the ground and laid her body to rest.

Her grandson John, now a pastor, wore a dark suit and carried a black Bible. He spoke these words over the casket: "In sure and certain hope of the resurrection to eternal life through our Lord Jesus Christ, we commend to Almighty God our sister, Elizabeth; and we commit her body to the ground. Earth to earth, dust to dust."

I looked at the crowd of people who'd gathered with us beside her grave. It was mostly family—my uncle, cousins, and Mum's closest friends—and I thought, *I don't really know these people.* I saw tears and genuine compassion and wondered what I'd missed, having rarely spent time with our extended family when we were growing up. Now I felt regret for that.

When a friend reached to steady my brother, the simple act shook me. We didn't do that in our family. We stood alone.

I watched as the first shovel moved over the casket and felt as if the dirt was burying my mother and her secrets.

❧

When I returned to the States, I found that my mother's death had unsettled me in ways that didn't make sense. Someone had pulled the rug out from under my feet, exposing all the secrets and lies I'd hidden for years—secrets and lies I believed about myself for too long.

For as long as I can remember, from the days of bruised knees and cartoon pajamas, I grew up believing that my dad's death was my fault. What's worse, we never talked about it. And so, as most children would, I lived with my own bare-bones version of the story, which went like this: My father had a brain aneurysm that impacted his personality; he went from being a warm, funny dad to an unpredictable stranger. When I was only five, he tried to bring his cane down on my skull. I screamed, he fell, and Mum dialed 911. Dad was taken away to the Ayrshire Lunatic Asylum. He escaped one night and drowned himself in the river, and I felt responsible for his death.

I grew up full of shame, believing I was a terrible person. I was a disgrace to the family. I was terrified of anger, and when anyone raised their voice, I became five years old again, fearing for my own life. I grew up fiercely self-protective and struggled to connect with anyone. And though I'd talked about some of these issues with a counselor, though I'd tried to deal with the shame, my mum's recent death shook things loose in me, things I didn't even know were there. I found myself in an unending cycle of anger and sadness. There was an overwhelming sense that we never said things to each other that might have brought deeper healing.

And this is what I've found to be true, though it took me years to discover it: When we don't say the true things, the things that might free us from secrets and lies, the poison seeps out of our lives and into the lives of others. Then anger and sadness surface when you least expect it. I know this because it happened to me, and the person in my line of fire was, of all people, my son, Christian.

When we don't say the true things, the things that might free us from secrets and lies, the poison seeps out of our lives and into the lives of others.

For their sophomore year at Texas A&M, Christian and three of his friends had rented an unfurnished house. The three other moms and I decided to split the list of basics that our boys would need. One mom found a dining-room table and chairs, one a vacuum cleaner and some basic kitchen appliances, and one a coffee table and barbeque grill. (Apparently that's a necessity for boys in Texas.) Barry and I were to find a sofa and an American flag for the front door.

Christian decided to drive to the house a couple of weeks before the fall semester began so he could get the house keys as soon as they were available. He was very excited and asked us if we'd come with him. If you have a child in college, particularly an only child, you understand this: if your child invites you to go anywhere, you accept.

We loaded as much of Christian's stuff into our car as we could and made the three-hour trip. We picked up the keys, the garage-door openers, and the welcome package. We drove to a furniture store and found a nice sofa; and after texting pictures of it to the other boys and their moms for approval, we bought it. Christian and Barry took me back to the house while they went off to track down the flag and a few other things on his list.

While they were gone I scrubbed the place down, emptying bathroom cabinets where the previous renters had left half-empty tubes of toothpaste and used floss. Once I had cleaned as much as I could, I went from room to room praying God's protection and grace over these four young men. I took some oil and anointed the front doorpost. Barry and Christian returned, and we all drove back to Dallas. It was the best of weekends.

The following week we received a phone call. Christian's bed was in stock and was ready for delivery. I couldn't go with him—I was taping a television show that week—but Barry said he'd go. The night before they left, Barry and Christian took our three dogs for a walk. When they returned, Barry came to our bedroom upset.

"What's wrong?" I asked.

"Christian really hurt me," he said. "He wants to know if I have to stay with him at the house. I was only going to help him, but he wants me to stay at a hotel. I'm not sure I'll even go now."

That's when the anger and sadness spilled out across the bedroom.

We've spoiled this child!

He takes everything for granted!

He can't wait to get away from us, but not until we've given him everything he wants!

I should have known that what I was feeling had little to do with Christian and more to do with the loss of my mum. I was still reeling from that loss and hadn't begun to sort out all the emotions. But instead of asking myself why I felt such uncontrolled anger, instead of taking an honest look at what was going on inside of me, I took it out on Christian. A few moments later Christian came up to see if his dad was okay, but before he had a chance to say anything, I lit into him.

"You really hurt your dad! We do so much for you, and you just take it for granted. Do you know how much money we've spent on you?"

On and on, my words flew like bullets from an automatic weapon. After I'd said all the unkind, untrue things, it felt as if all the air had been sucked out of the room. Barry stood, speechless. Christian looked as if I had just mortally wounded him.

"I'm sorry," Christian said, then he went back downstairs.

Silence. All I could hear was my heart thumping in my chest. I sat for a moment, the tears welling up.

Lord, what's wrong with me? I prayed. *In one moment I changed from a loving mother to a monster.*

I sat in my bedroom, silent. My heart thumped and thumped and thumped. I knew I'd lost it. I had overreacted and sprayed my son with the unresolved anger and shame of my own childhood. My mind returned to an old, shameful thought: *If only I hadn't screamed when my dad tried to bring his cane down on my head, maybe my dad would still be here. It was my screams that brought my mum running*

Your reaction

has little to do with

what's in front of you

and everything

to do with what's

inside you.

into the room and set everything else in motion. I should have run instead. I should have hidden. If only I hadn't looked at him as if he was a monster, as if I didn't want to be around him, maybe he wouldn't have drowned himself.

These were the lies I'd told myself year after year after year, and instead of dealing with them, I let them fester, let them gain force and steam and magma until I erupted on Christian.

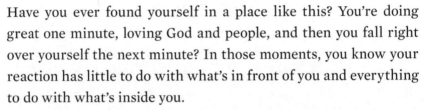

Have you ever found yourself in a place like this? You're doing great one minute, loving God and people, and then you fall right over yourself the next minute? In those moments, you know your reaction has little to do with what's in front of you and everything to do with what's inside you.

The truth is, I lived most of my life walling off parts of myself that I thought were unacceptable, stuffing away all the fear, shame, and pain. I convinced myself that I should never talk about them, not even with God. My silence, however, isolated me and made me desperately lonely.

I grew up believing that I had to hide who I really was because that little girl was a bad girl, bad enough to make her dad want to kill both her and himself. Throughout seminary, a singing career, hosting my own television show, and years of speaking at women's conferences, I wanted to be okay. I thought I was. Then one phone call—*Mum's gone, Sheila*—threatened my sense of "being okay." The secrets and lies spilled out in ways that hurt the people I loved most.

Perhaps there was a solution, a way forward. Maybe there was a way to live the beautiful message of Christ, even in the middle of my mess. But how?

Reflection

Have you ever found yourself in one of those moments when your reaction was out of proportion to the event that precipitated it?

I encourage you to pay attention to these reactions. Take time to sit with them. What's happening in those moments?

Don't condemn yourself for what's been locked inside. The enemy of our souls condemns, but the Holy Spirit urges us to confess, leading us to healing. Read the scripture below. What does it say about facing down our inner messes?

> "A bruised reed he will not break,
> and a smoldering wick he will not snuff out."
>
> —Isaiah 42:3 NIV

Chapter 3

∽∾

The Walls We Build

Truth, like gold, is to be obtained not by its growth,
but by washing away from it all that is not gold.

—LEO TOLSTOY

Saying good-bye to my mother left me feeling profoundly sad and desperately anxious, and I wanted to understand why. She had lived a good, long life. She'd loved God, her church home, and her family. Now she was finally free from sickness and pain. Shouldn't I be rejoicing in her freedom? Why, then, was I in such pain? Why did it feel as though I had a lead weight on my chest? Why did I feel panic churning just below the surface? It didn't make sense.

I grew up with a profound sense of the reality of death. I was five years old when Dad committed suicide. I don't remember who told me that Dad was dead. He was just gone. We didn't talk about how we felt after his death, and this became the pattern for the following fifty-five years of living. So why now—as we should have been celebrating a godly woman who lived a full life—did I feel as if I was about to fall apart in grief?

The day after Mum's funeral, I sat cross-legged on the guest-room bed in my sister's house, computer open, searching Scripture for a verse on sadness. Frustration grew as I found myself scrolling across page after page of verses recognizing the sadness of life followed by the hope we have in Christ. Don't get me wrong: Hope is a beautiful thing. I am alive because of that hope. But in that moment, I needed to sit in the truth of the present before rushing to the hope of tomorrow.

I considered a conversation I had with one of our producers on my television show years before. I wanted to invite guests who hadn't received the answers they'd prayed for. That's the reality for many of us. I wanted to explore the disappointment that haunts even the most ardent follower of God. The response was disheartening. "That's not faith building," I was told. The implication was clear—that we needed to share stories of people who received the miracles they prayed for, which would build up the faith of others who had not. That felt cruel to me. I imagined a mom watching a story about a child being healed and wondering why her child was still sick. Was it her fault? Didn't she have enough faith?

I know the truth now—pretending that something doesn't exist doesn't make it go away. Skimming over pain doesn't build faith; it builds shame and isolation. If you're hurting or disappointed or angry or sad but you see everyone else around you acting just fine—even those who are facing difficult circumstances—you begin to wonder: *What's wrong with me?*

That's what I felt when I went back to the cemetery late on the day we buried my mum. Grass had been placed over the grave, and someone had arranged the flowers in front of it—white lilies, cream tulips, and yellow roses. I wanted to scream aloud, "Why do we do this? Why do we cover up every gaping hole of disappointment and make it look pretty?"

This tension, this pain . . . I felt it that night, looking down at the place where Mum was laid to rest. It took me back to a night when I was about ten years old. I woke up needing to use the restroom.

When I passed my mum's bedroom I saw light seeping from the crack under the door. I placed my hand on the knob, but before I turned it, something stopped me. I heard her muffled crying. She was sobbing into some fabric, perhaps her pillow. I'd never seen my mum cry, and instinctively I knew that she didn't want me to, so I slipped down onto the carpet on the other side of the door and cried too. That was one of my earliest lessons about sorrow and grief. Sorrow was not to be shared; it was private. So I learned to cry alone.

I still wish I'd been able to sit with my mum that night, or at other times when she struggled with the pain. I wish I'd been able to sit with her, not just as my mum, but as a sister in Christ. I wish we could have pushed beyond the first layer of loss and disappointment and into the deeper stuff underneath.

How did she grieve?
Did she talk to God about the pain?
Did she feel as if God abandoned her on that violent day when it took four men to carry my raging dad out of our house?
Was she ever glad my dad was gone?
Did that make her feel like a traitor?

For so many years, I assumed she didn't want to have those conversations. I now think I was wrong.

In the fall of 1992, I had been in the psychiatric hospital for two weeks. My counselor asked Mum if she would be willing to fly over and sit in on some of my sessions. Mum agreed, and I booked her flight.

In my counselor's office, I sat on the couch, Mum in an oversized chair facing both of us. My heart thumped inside my chest, and I thought I might throw up.

The counselor faced my mum and said, "Sheila has something she wants to tell you."

Mum looked at me. I offered a silent prayer—*Jesus, please help me. I can't do this. We won't survive this.*

"I . . . I'm sorry. I'm so, so sorry for what I did. I'm sorry that I took Dad away from you and ruined your life. Please forgive me."

I fell onto the floor with my head in my hands. I don't know what I expected, but it wasn't the cry I heard coming from my mother. She poured out a primal cry, a deep-inside-the-secret-well cry. "It wasn't your fault," she finally said when she could speak. "It was mine."

In the presence of the counselor that day, we exposed our wounds and bled together. Some of that conversation will stay between Mum and me, but it was the first time we really talked about Dad even though he'd been gone for thirty years. I learned that day that she'd carried an unbearable burden, believing for decades that she had allowed my dad to stay in our home too long. The conversation wasn't long; it was just a moment. And it didn't open up an ongoing and unguarded dialogue that would continue in the years that followed.

Opening up cost her a lot—old wounds torn open, her generational privacy. It also showed me that for as long as I had carried the shame of my dad's death, Mum had carried the guilt. And that's when I realized that most of us hide our pain. It's also when I first learned these two truths: Lies breed in silence, and silence is deadly. Though speaking the truth can be painful, sharing the secrets can bring healing.

*Though speaking the truth can be painful,
sharing the secrets can bring healing.*

Not all loss or disappointment weighs the same. Some things are easier to carry than others. I know this now. And I think that's what Paul meant when he told those in Galatia who loved Christ to "bear one another's burdens" (Gal. 6:2 NKJV). A few verses later, though, he says that "each one shall bear his own load" (Gal. 6:5 NKJV).

Upon first reading, the passage is a bit confusing. Paul appears to contradict himself. How can we bear each other's burdens if we're all supposed to bear our own loads? But digging a bit deeper brings clarity. I've discovered that the Greek word for *burdens* is *báros*, which refers to a heavy load or a ship's load. The Greek word used for *load* is *phortíon*, which is used exclusively in the New Testament to refer to the load Christ speaks of—a load only He can help us carry: "For my yoke is easy, and my burden is light" (Matt. 11:30 ESV).

I suppose I've stumbled into this truth over the years. There are some losses that feel like a ship's load, like more than we can carry. That's when we desperately need each other, I think. When we're left to carry that kind of burden, or *báros*, alone, it changes us.

I grew up carrying my own ship's load. I was taught—though not explicitly—that I didn't really need anyone to help me carry the loss of my dad. I didn't allow myself to feel sad or mad or anything else that felt overwhelming, because sharing emotional weight was not acceptable. I didn't think that was strange. I just thought it was my reserved Scottish personality. I could hurt for you if you were in pain, and I might even help you carry your burden; but I'd never ask for your help in carrying mine. I was self-sufficient, if hidden.

I know now that I built a secret place inside myself, a place where I thought no person, no pain, no emotional threat could reach me. It was a hiding place. Whatever that structure was, it showed cracks back in the psych ward, but the whole thing began to give way beside my mum's grave all these years later. What I didn't realize was that the brokenness of my childhood had followed me into my adult life, and I carried it with me, deep inside the cellar of my soul. Now, that brokenness and all the pain began dismantling the cellar walls from the inside out.

I have always needed a community around me—we all do—but it was the thing I was most afraid of. It's why I hid, even when surrounded by community. It's why I guarded that secret cellar. I wondered: *What if I let you see the real me? What if I let you into my innermost thoughts and feelings and you took a long, hard look? Would you see a scared, broken little girl? Would you see someone who didn't have it all together, who didn't know how to trust the Jesus she loved to preach? Would you turn and walk away? What would I do then? What would I do without my hiding place?*

You would think that within Christian community—specifically within the church—I could have confessed my shame, my panic, my fear. But I knew that sometimes our Christian community is the crucible where shame is born. Many of you also know this sad truth. Too often, sharing secrets and shame in the church begets more shame, which leads to more secret-keeping. That is tragic. We survive, cut off from the very help and healing we need.

The Bible describes many people who lived shame-filled lives until they looked into the eyes of Jesus. In His eyes, their shame was met with fiery love and burned to ash. There were so many women who were shamed by their culture but were restored by His love: the prostitute, the woman at the well, the woman who was caught in adultery and thrown to the ground at Jesus' feet. He saw them in some of their worst moments and loved them.

That's still true. Christ hates the sin and shame that devastates— especially, perhaps, the secret sin and shame—but He is crazy passionate about us. The devastating message of shame is that we *are* something wrong, but Christ nailed that lie to a tree more than two thousand years ago: "Those who look to him for help will be radiant with joy; no shadow of shame will darken their faces" (Ps. 34:5).

Christ nailed our sin and shame to the cross, and in so doing, He brought it out into the open and released it of its power over us. Christ made it our mission to love our fellow shame carriers, the secret bearers, the same way He did. He made it our mission to love them back to life. It's our calling to let them know that shame no longer lives. It died on a cross two thousand years ago, and we need not resurrect it. We can help them carry their loads without adding the weight of shame.

Christ *nailed*

our sin and shame

to the cross,

and in so doing,

He *brought* it out

into the open and

released it of its

power over us.

The relentless love of Christ pursues us through all our secret shame. I can see that now. Looking back over my history, I see the people He put in my path to speak truth to the lies, to unveil the secrets that kept me isolated and so lonely, to help me carry the load without shame. I am grateful for the gentleness of His mercy in unexpected places.

❧

A year before Mum's death, I was sitting in a departure lounge waiting for my flight to board when that dreaded announcement graced our ears: "The 3:30 p.m. flight to Dallas, Texas, will now depart at 5:40 p.m. Thank you for your patience."

I looked at my fellow passengers and questioned the announcer's gratitude for the passengers' "patience." It was our flight's third delay, and tempers were flaring. I picked up my briefcase once again and returned to the coffee shop where I had spent much of the last two hours. I ordered a cup of tea and was settling in to read my newspaper when I became aware of someone standing in front of me. I looked up. A woman about my age, tall and slim with short blonde hair, smiled and asked, "Would you mind if I joined you for a moment?"

"No, of course not," I said.

"I heard you speak at a conference," she said. "We have similar stories."

"When was that?" I asked.

"It was last year, in California," she said. "It led to this."

She pulled up the sleeve of her sweater to reveal a tattoo on her wrist. It was a semicolon.

"May I ask what that means?" I said.

She looked down at it and rubbed her fingers over the black ink.

"It's about choosing to live one more day," she said. "I'm part of a movement."

"What's the movement?" I asked.

"It's called Project Semicolon." She explained that it was a community of support for those who struggle with thoughts of self-harm and suicide. For those who battle mental illness or addiction. It was a community for those who needed to share the truth. She'd been at the conference hosted by Saddleback Church, she said, and it had changed her life. "I joined Project Semicolon after I heard you speak."

I remembered that conference well. Kay Warren had invited me to be a keynote speaker at the annual Church and Mental Health Symposium, a conference rising from the ashes of Kay and Rick's son Matthew Warren's suicide. I remember being unusually nervous as I flew out to speak that first night. I wasn't quite sure what I could add. The lineup of speakers was impressive and intimidating— United States Surgeon General Vice Admiral Vivek Murthy; Paul Summergrad, former head of the American Psychiatric Association; former congressman Patrick Kennedy; and many, many more.

I was the speaker on the opening night, which I was grateful for because it meant I didn't have to follow any of the other specialized presenters. I remember my opening line so well. It's something I couldn't have said for most of my life.

"Good evening. My name is Sheila Walsh, and I am profoundly grateful for the gift of mental illness. It means that I can look into the eyes of someone else who is suffering and say: me too."

Me too.

Such little words. But how I would have welcomed hearing them from someone in the weeks before I was hospitalized! In those days the church rarely addressed any area of mental illness.

I looked at the woman across from me in the airport coffee shop. "So, what does the semicolon mean?" I asked.

She looked down at her wrist again and said, "A semicolon is used when an author could've ended a sentence but chose not to. I am the author, and the sentence is my life."[1]

She told me that when she raises her hands in worship, that little tattoo becomes an offering to God, a daily acknowledgment of her brokenness and her faith.

"That's powerful," I said.

"I need to go now. My flight's boarding," she said, picking up her backpack.

I thanked her for sharing her story. And I meant it. I needed to hear her words.

After she left I thought about the little tattoo on her wrist. What was it about that symbol that helped her so much? Perhaps it reminds her to fight through the darkest nights of depression. It gives her something to focus on. It tells her to hold on. It's a tangible declaration to her weary soul that her story is not over yet even when her mind tells her it should be.

Further, perhaps it lets her know she is not alone. It reminds her of the community around her who says "me too." Shame thrives in hiding and solitude. It whispers,

You're all alone.
You'll never be enough.
You'll never change.

Freedom begins in a community of "me too" people, people committed to helping you carry your burden. Being part of Project Semicolon has given her that kind of community. They don't understand because they are experts. They understand because they're honest about their own suffering, and they help her combat the lies. They help her see the truth about herself, and they accept her just as she is. That kind of community deprives shame of the oxygen that keeps it alive.

Speaking the truth about her life to those who understand her path has given her strength to keep walking.

After she left, I sat and considered Christ's encounter with Zacchaeus, a man despised by everyone who knew him. He was Jewish, yes, but he was also a tax collector for the Roman occupiers.

The Romans gave this unsavory job to local recruits and allowed them to keep a percentage of whatever they collected. Zacchaeus and his colleagues took more than what was owed. They were parasites living off the vulnerability of their own people. When Christ decided to share a meal with Zacchaeus, the people were horrified. How could Jesus spend time with a man who was bleeding them dry?

This was His response: "The Son of Man came to seek and save those who are lost" (Luke 19:10). I considered the verse and thought about the study I'd done on it years ago. The word used here for *lost* means "destroyed, ruined, broken beyond repair."

I thought about the woman, about her semicolon tattoo. I thought about Jesus, who didn't come for those who are doing-just-fine-thank-you. He came to save those who were and are willing to acknowledge they are broken beyond repair. And even now, in His tender way, He comes to the doors of our hidden places and invites Himself in for supper.

Jesus comes to us in the secret shadows and bids us into the light. He wants to be in communion with us, wants to help carry the load of the pain and shame we secret away in isolation.

I don't think I'm the only one who has constructed walls around parts of myself. We all know that pain is part of life, but when too much of it happens all at once—when it happens too early in life or when we feel helpless to combat it—the pain can make us believe we don't want to go on. It's why we build a secret place inside ourselves where it can hang out. The pain might follow us there, but we believe it can't hurt us as much if it's walled up. And we falsely think that the world can't see it either.

We can pretend that everything is okay. And perhaps that's a sort of saving grace for some of us as children. When I think of the stories women have shared with me through the years—stories of the worst kind of abuse and betrayal—I've wondered how they've made it. Perhaps some have survived by burying the pain deep inside, but I believe now that others have discovered the beauty of living open, yet broken, with Christ.

My new friend with the tattoo doesn't pretend that her pain is gone but brings it into the light of a crucified Savior. He helps her carry it with hands scarred by love. His resounding "Yes!" to the Father's plan to save us took Him down a brutal bloody path, but it gave life to each one of us who will say yes to Christ and no to the lies that would keep us hidden.

Reflections

I know your story is different from mine, but pain is pain and you are not alone.

In Luke 19, Christ makes His way into Jerusalem on the back of a donkey. The crowds welcome Him with open arms, shouting, "Blessed is the king who comes in the name of the Lord! Peace in heaven and glory in the highest!" (v. 38 NIV).

Then Luke tells us that as Christ looked over the Holy City, He wept "because you did not recognize it when God visited you" (v. 44).

Luke moves away from that panoramic picture and focuses on the weeping face of Christ. Why do you think Christ wept in that moment?

I wonder if Christ ever weeps over us when—even as we raise our voices in worship—our hearts, our shame, our pain is hidden? Is there something you have hidden away inside that you need to bring into the light of Christ?

My friend Ann Voskamp inks a little cross on her wrist each morning as a reminder of the One who was wounded for her so she doesn't have to wound herself. What would help you to remember the relentless love of Christ during the messy moments of life?

> God is our refuge and strength,
> a very present help in trouble.
>
> —Psalm 46:1 ESV

Chapter 4

❧

You Don't Have to Hide

In a room where people unanimously maintain a conspiracy of silence, one word of truth sounds like a pistol shot.

—CZESLAW MILOSZ

Two days before Mum died, Barry and I were preparing for a trip to California. We'd booked flights and a hotel by our favorite beach to celebrate our summer birthdays. I was excited because it had been a long time since we'd taken a vacation. On the morning of our departure, I woke at five, poured myself a cup of coffee, and let the dogs out. I sat in the cool of the morning air, the moon still in place, enjoying the silence. "Be still and know that I am God," I whispered as a reminder.

As I sat in the silence that morning, I had a strong sense that God was telling me we shouldn't take the trip. It didn't make any sense, though. We both needed a break. God knew that, but I couldn't shake the conviction. When Barry woke up I told him the news, and he said, "If God's saying don't go, we won't go." Two days later, Frances called and I flew to Scotland to tend to my mum's passing.

About a month later, when I was back home in Dallas, I had only just begun to process all my emotions. We were preparing to send Christian back to college, and we had so many commitments to keep. As Labor Day approached, I was tired, emotionally spent, and desperate to get away. We'd lost our deposit on the hotel in California, and after getting Christian settled into his new house, cash was tight. So I asked God if He could make a way. I prayed and I waited.

A couple of days later, a friend mentioned that the people who had booked their condo by the ocean on North Padre Island, Texas, might be canceling their reservation. If they did, he said, he wanted me to use it.

That night I prayed, *If this would be a good thing, Lord, please open the door. If not, slam it closed.* The following morning, my friend called and said it was all mine. It was the open door I was waiting for, and I was filled with excitement and gratitude. I would be staying ocean-side for a week, rent-free, and it was in Texas, so I could drive! It seemed like grace upon grace. No makeup, no high heels—just T-shirts and a ball cap.

Barry knew that I needed a little time by myself, so he offered to stay home with the dogs while I rested and prayed. I Google-mapped my journey and realized that the drive would be about six and a half hours—uninterrupted time to think. He kissed me good-bye as I set off just after nine the following morning. After a stop at the first Cracker Barrel for an audiobook and a Diet Coke, I was good to go.

An hour into the journey, things began to go wrong. The air-conditioning in my car quit on a day stretching into the high nineties. I'd only had the car for six months, so it didn't make much sense. I turned the dial to max to see if it might kick back in, but it didn't. I turned it off and kept driving for a bit, but after an hour, sweat was dripping off my forehead and into my eyes. I rolled down the windows, hoping that the fresh air would dry me out. And it did—that is, until the storm hit about thirty minutes later. Out of nowhere, the sky dumped buckets of hot water, and before I could get my window rolled up, I was soaked to the skin. Traffic came to a stop, and cars turned on their hazard lights because the downpour made it almost impossible to see.

I alternated between windows down and large buckets of water coming in, and windows up and large buckets of sweat pouring down. It was a vehicular Sophie's Choice. I called Barry and told him about my predicament with a long way to drive still ahead of me. He told me to sit tight—which was not a problem, as traffic had come to a complete stop. He said he'd work on it. What seemed like hours later, he called and told me that the local car dealer at Padre had one service appointment left before the Labor Day holiday. It was mine if I could have the car there by nine o'clock the following morning. Grateful, I accepted.

Nine hours later I entered the condo development, soaking wet and tired. That's when I noticed that the truck that had been behind me for the last two miles also pulled into the development right behind me. As quick as I could, I parked in front of my friend's condo, bolted from the car, and hustled through the front door. Once inside, I peeked out the kitchen window to see if the truck had parked in front of one of the other units. It hadn't. It was in the space beside mine.

I was nervous being all by myself, but for all I knew, one of the passengers lived next door. Maybe they were simply finishing up a conversation, or perhaps they were on the FBI's Most Wanted list. I made myself a cup of tea and waited. The hours passed until, at about three o'clock in the morning, the truck left and I went to bed.

The following morning, I brewed some coffee and got into the car for my appointment at the car dealership. But as soon as I started the engine, I discovered that my air conditioner had fixed itself during the night. Thankful for the reprieve, I canceled my appointment and drove straight to the local drugstore. I bought a towel, a book, a bottle of water, and a beach chair.

Less than an hour later, I crested the top of the sand dunes and gazed at the ocean in front of me. I walked to a deserted area of sand several feet above the waterline and situated my chair and belongings. As soon as my body hit the chair, however, it collapsed on top of me. I was trapped—quite literally. Apart from a large breedless dog who had bounded up out of nowhere and kept licking my feet, I couldn't see anyone else on this stretch of beach. And I couldn't figure how to get out of my predicament. By the time I dug myself out, my legs were bruised and scraped, and it had started to rain. My canine friend wagged his tail, and I left him the soggy towel before I headed back to the condo. The week was not going as planned, and after another spate of mishaps—which would take too long to describe—I decided to abandon the trip and go home.

I threw my bags into the car and began the journey back to Dallas. An hour into the trip, the air-conditioning went out again. This time I didn't bother rolling down the windows. Instead, I just kept going—a sweaty, defeated beast. When the first storm hit, I thought, *Ha! You thought you'd get me again, did you? But my windows are all the way up!* Unfortunately, the sunroof was not. By the time I got it closed, I was once again a soppy mess. I got home at midnight looking like a drowned rat. Barry met me at the door with a stack of towels and a cup of tea.

Nothing had turned out the way I thought it would. It hadn't been the worst experience of my life, and it certainly wasn't the end of the world, but it had been disappointing. It also felt scarier than that. It felt like a tipping point. Like the childhood game of blocks, the one in which you tell yourself, *I can put one more on,* right before the whole thing comes tumbling down. My experience hadn't been a life-and-death event that pushed me over the edge, but it was a defining moment when nothing in life—not even a spiritual retreat— seemed to make sense. I had believed that God had opened this door for me, even asking Him to shut it according to His will. I felt raw, exhausted, disappointed with God, and scared. That's when the old feelings of depression set in.

I suppose I thought I had this whole depression thing under

control. It wasn't healed, but it was manageable. I had agreed to speak about mental health and depression at the Church and Mental Health Symposium because I believed that the worst of my depression was behind me thanks to a system that had worked. I took my meds faithfully. I tried to eat well and get exercise. I had solid community—Barry and my three closest friends Lisa Harper, Sandi Patty, and Lisa Bevere, who knew me so well. If I was having a bad day, I could text them and they'd respond right away.

Do you want to do a conference call?
We're on our knees on your behalf.

It felt as if I'd found a good shelf to land on—perhaps not perfect, but secure. And now something as small as a disappointing trip was making me lose my footing. Of course it wasn't the trip—not really—just as it wasn't about Christian when he'd asked his father to stay in a hotel. These were the frustrations that God used to get my attention, and just as I'd lashed out at Christian, I lashed out at God.

That trip? It was a total waste of time! I wasn't asking for a lot, just a little break. You could have shut the door. I would have been fine with that. After Mum dying and Christian going back to college, would it have been too much to ask to let me rest by the beach for a few days? Why couldn't You have made this work? I'm sad and I'm angry and I'm so tired!

And this is what I felt God saying to me: "I know. I'm sorry. Just pour it all out. Tell Me everything."

So I did. As far back as I could remember.

I dared to tell the whole truth out loud to God. I let Him into my secret place where I'd hidden my emotions. I felt bone-weary of being "the good girl," the one who said the right things no matter how hard life was. I considered my emotions in earnest for the first time, and I poured it all out.

You could have stopped my dad from killing himself.
You could at least have protected me from his rage.
Do You know how much I hated myself because I lived and he died?
Do You know how ashamed I've been all my life?
Do You know how scared I am right now?
Do You know how small I feel?
Do You know that I've never felt as if I belong anywhere?
Do You know how much I miss my mum?

I poured it all out until there was nothing left. I cried and cried until every tear was gone. Scriptures that I'd shared with others when they were hurting came to my mind, including: "When the righteous cry for help, the LORD hears and delivers them out of all their troubles. The LORD is near to the brokenhearted and saves the crushed in spirit. Many are the afflictions of the righteous, but the LORD delivers him out of them all" (Ps. 34:17–19 ESV).

Instead of finding comfort, I challenged this promise.

But You didn't deliver my dad. You didn't deliver me. Scripture says that the Lord delivers us out of all our troubles. You didn't do that!

Silence fell. I was always afraid that the truth would leave me alone, but that day I found that I'd never felt less alone in my life. I discovered a new insight: Christ is with me when I confess the whole truth, and He is lifting the weight.

I sat up as the stillness washed over me. Then, I picked up my Bible and my journal. I felt a pulling, felt drawn to a story I knew well but didn't like at all.

In the past, I'd found the story of Abraham and Isaac cruel. In Genesis 22 God asks Abraham to take Isaac, the son that he and Sarah had waited so long for, to the peak of Mount Moriah to slaughter him in sacrifice.

Why would God do that? Why would He make them wait until Sarah was ninety years old, well beyond the possibility of conceiving a child, only to ask Abraham to kill their son? And what made it

Christ is with

me when I

confess

the whole truth,

and He is

lifting

the weight.

even more confusing to me was that God knew all along that He'd step in at the last minute and save Isaac, that He'd provide an alternative sacrifice right before Abraham's knife pierced Isaac's heart. I believed God did that to reward Abraham's obedience—at least that's what I'd always been taught—which played right into my old belief of "performing" for God. Doesn't God want us all to jump through hoops just to prove that we love Him?

I read the passage over and over because I knew that the Holy Spirit was trying to illuminate something that I was missing. So I read, and I read, and I read. In fact, for most of that day that's all I did. Then I turned to another familiar story, and slowly I began to understand. The beauty of it almost broke my heart.

I've heard sermons comparing the story of Abraham and Isaac to Jesus, saying that God spared Isaac but didn't spare His own Son, but there's so much more to it. As I read the story of Christ's crucifixion, the parallels leaped off the page.

Abraham placed the wood for the sacrificial pyre on Isaac's back (Gen. 22:6).
    Christ carried the cross on His back up the hill of His sacrifice (John 19:17).

Isaac cried out to his father, asking where the sacrifice was for the offering (Gen. 22:7).
    Christ cried out to His Father, asking why He'd turned His back on Him, the sacrifice (Matt. 27:46).

Isaac escaped death after a three-day journey (Gen. 22:4).
    Christ escaped death when He rose from the dead on the third day (Matt. 28:5–6).

When Isaac asked what the sacrifice would be, Abraham told Isaac that God would provide a lamb (Gen. 22:8).
    God provided Christ, the perfect, sinless Lamb (John 1:29).

There are more parallels in the stories, but there is one powerful distinction that caught my attention. Abraham took his son to the top of Mount Moriah, but he brought his son back down again. Christ walked up that hill to Calvary, but He didn't come back down—at least not immediately. On that hill Christ shed His blood to save every broken one of us.

I'd completely missed what it means to be delivered, to be saved. Up until then, I'd thought salvation meant that we were fixed. Wow, how small my view! I put aside everything that made sense to me and took another look. As I sat in my Father's presence that day, I saw Jesus on every page of the Word of God. What happened with Abraham and Isaac on Mount Moriah all those years ago wasn't a cruel test; it was the very embodiment of the promise of deliverance. And my deliverance—our deliverance—was made possible by the Lamb of God. I'd never seen it so clearly before.

I sat in the epiphany. I still didn't quite understand my waterlogged trip, but I believe it was an invitation from my Father.

Come on, Sheila. Tell Me what you're really feeling. You don't have to hide anymore. I will be with you in every hurt, upset, and disappointment. Confess it all to Me. I am your Safe Place.

That's when it began to become clear. I didn't have to hide my true self from God. I could lay it on the altar and trust that I'd be delivered. I could find my true self by trusting in God's ongoing and present salvation.

Ultimately, I think this was the panic I felt as I stood by my mother's grave—had she wanted to tell me more? Did she ever get to pour out the whole truth to God? Did she find deliverance? If she didn't, could I? Would I ever get to tell the whole truth? What would God do if I poured it out? What if I admitted that I blamed myself for my dad's death? What if I admitted that I blamed God for it? Would He turn His back on me if I didn't perform, if I didn't say all the right things about death? Would He deliver me from the shame, guilt, and lies?

Even as I'm writing this, I think of mothers who've lost a child.

I cannot imagine the pain of such loss, and there are no words to soothe that kind of outrageous grief. How does your heart ever heal? How do your arms ever recover? One moment you're holding this precious gift of life, and the next it's snatched away. If you have suffered this kind of loss, my heart grieves for you. Whether you got to hold your child or you lost a little one through miscarriage, a part of your heart no longer lives on this earth. And what do you say to God about this grief? Do you dare confront it, confront Him? Could He deliver you from your anger, your grief, your pain?

Not all losses weigh the same. Some disappointments may seem small measured against others, so we don't bring them into the light. You didn't get the promotion you hoped for, or someone else's child was given the part in the play that yours worked so hard for. You went out of your way to help someone else, but they didn't even seem to notice. They're not life-changing losses, but they are very real disappointments. Instead of speaking those out loud, though, we often stuff them inside because we don't want to seem small or petty before God. But hear this truth: Nothing that affects you is petty to God. He loves you and cares about everything that affects you. He wants to deliver you, to bring you present salvation.

But hear this truth: Nothing
that affects you is petty to God.

I don't know what losses you've had in your life. I don't know what you're walking through right now, but I want to say this: Don't hurry through it, and don't hide the pain. Don't let anyone tell you to get over it, and don't hide it in secret, thinking the pain won't find you there. It will. I promise. Wouldn't you rather confess it to God, to feel Him taking your load and delivering you?

God will never be offended by your honest, gut-level grief or anger. I think we only offend Him when we hide our pain, when we pretend that we can save or shield ourselves from it. Trust Him with the real you, all of you. Pour out your heart, your tears, and your disappointment. God will never run from the real you. He will pull you close.

Maybe you don't know where to start. If you don't know how to invite Him into the pain, perhaps we can practice together. Speak your pain out loud. Get used to the sound of your own voice telling the truth. You don't have to be afraid of being broken. We'll always be broken this side of heaven, but that brokenness can only follow us so far. Speak and speak and speak your pain until you've said the things you need to say, until it's second nature to hear the sound of your voice confessing. Then, pause and reflect on this pain. Confess it to God. Invite Him into your innermost heart, the place you keep your pain locked away. Invite Him, then listen to His invitation of deliverance.

You can trust Me, even if you don't understand. When the tears have dried and you have no words left, place your hand in Mine. I love you. I will deliver you. I Am your Safe Place.

Reflection

Confession is part of how Christ taught us to pray: "Forgive us our debts, as we also have forgiven our debtors" (Matt. 6:12 ESV).

As a child I learned to say the Lord's Prayer, which is found in Matthew 6. For a long time, my confessions were simple; they never came from the cellar of my soul, but only from the surface layer of my heart. I never felt free or whole, not until I began the intentional daily confession of all that I know to be true about myself. Frederick Buechner wrote: "To confess your sins to God is not to tell God anything God doesn't already know. Until you confess them, however, they are the abyss between you. When you confess them, they become the Golden Gate Bridge."[1]

I encourage you to begin this daily practice. Rather than alienate you from God, confession will bring you into a fresh depth of His sweet presence. Find a quiet place. Be still. Invite the Holy Spirit to reveal your sin.

I often use the words of David when I confess: "Search me, O God, and know my heart; test me and know my anxious thoughts. Point out anything in me that offends you, and lead me along the path of everlasting life" (Ps. 139:23–24).

It might be helpful to write down the sins that you struggle most with. Pray for understanding and trust Christ for deliverance. Don't put *confession* on your to-do list. This is not one more thing to do; this is who we are in Christ.

> But if we confess our sins to him, he is faithful and just to forgive us our sins and to cleanse us from all wickedness.
>
> —1 John 1:9

Chapter 5

꩜

No More Bumper-Sticker Faith

The brain may take advice, but not the heart.

—TRUMAN CAPOTE, *OTHER VOICES, OTHER ROOMS*

I'm sorry for your loss," she said, refreshing her lipstick in the bathroom mirror.

"Thank you," I said.

"We don't live as those with no hope, dear," she added, placing her hand on my shoulder. Then she said, "We're so looking forward to hearing you speak tonight."

"Thank you," I said again. Then she was gone.

I looked at my face in the bathroom mirror. Did I look as if I was grieving? It was my first speaking engagement since Mum's funeral. Admittedly, I still felt a bit raw, but I'd never met the woman in the bathroom before and her comment, although kind, felt random. That night I was speaking at a banquet for some of the donors who support the work of LIFE Outreach International—the ministry with which I work.

LIFE Outreach International drills water wells in Africa, provides food for the poorest of the poor, and works with young boys and girls who've been trafficked in Thailand and Cambodia. It's a work that liberates girls from their living hell and brings them to a rescue center in the mountains of Thailand, a safe place of their own. I get to travel to all our projects and see with my own eyes what hope looks like.

When I came out of the bathroom, I saw one of our staff members standing in the hall and asked him if he knew who the woman was. He said that she and her husband have been very generous supporters for years.

"I wonder why she talked to me about grieving, though?" I asked.

"I believe they follow you on Facebook," he said with a smile.

Ah, Facebook. Suddenly it all made sense. Before I flew to Scotland I posted a photo of Mum on my Facebook page, asking those who followed me if they would pray for my family. I didn't read the responses until sometime later. Most of them were kind, a simple assurance of prayer support. Some went beyond that, though, and their words felt like instruction. One woman wrote, "Trusting you will see this time as a gift from God to reach your family members who are unsaved." The comment felt odd, and though I'm sure the heart behind her comment was well-intentioned, I wanted to say, "Do you know that all my family members follow me on Facebook too?" I also wanted her to know that saying good-bye to my mum didn't feel like a gift. It felt like a gift had been taken away.

Comment after comment streamed through my feed, but the one that bothered me most came from a woman who wrote, "Just think how God is going to use this next part of your story for His glory, Hallelujah. Our pain is His purpose." It read like the worst kind of bumper sticker. I wondered if she'd ever had any pain. I wondered if she had thought about what it would feel like to receive that advice if she had been the one to lose a dear family member. That's when I recalled some advice from my friend, Barbara Johnson: "When the pain is the freshest, the words should be the fewest." A woman left a heartbreaking response below the commenter's bumper-sticker comment. She said that she had just lost a son and didn't want God's purpose. Instead, she wanted her boy back.

I held my breath. I wanted to hold that woman. I wanted to sit with her in silence or tears for as long as she would let me. I wanted to tell her that her honest, simple statement of a mother's grief spoke more to me than all the platitudes in the world. I wanted to tell her that I believed her honest words were more of a sweet fragrance to God than pretend wholeness would ever be. Purpose is not a cure-all for pain.

Looking at those comments, I thought back to the lies I believed from childhood and how they impacted my relationship with God and others. I spent so much of my life trying to bury the grief in appropriate Christian platitudes—*Our pain is His purpose!*—or squeeze it into a mold that resembled something hopeful or some testimony of resurrection. But burying the grief in good Christian slogans is only an avoidance tactic, and avoiding the truth is still a lie. Lies can cripple even the strongest legs.

I grew up believing that if your own dad could turn on you, then so could your heavenly Dad. If I didn't want my heavenly Dad to turn on me, I'd better behave, look the part of the most joyous Christian, and never let Him down. If there was pain, it was best to keep it to myself; I wouldn't want anyone to think I wasn't a good Christian because I hurt or felt hopeless. What's more, I believed that pain creates walls between people, so I learned to be stronger on my own.

So many coping mechanisms, avoidance techniques, and lies. They kept me blind to where Christ was in the middle of my mess, where He was waiting for me to cry out for help, waiting for me to grieve. God had a rescue center waiting for me, His little girl, if only I'd been able to see it. But this is the beauty: sometimes, even when we try to avoid the truth, God uses the smallest hands to invite us into the safety of deliverance.

The one who took the first brick out of the wall between God and me was my son. To be precise, it was a memory of my son. Sitting there with those Facebook comments, those wounding words, I recalled carrying Christian through the Miami airport late one night. He must have been about eighteen months old. It had been a very long day, and he whispered in my ear, "Mommy, I've wet myself. Will you cover me?" I wrapped my coat around him and held him tight. He never saw the tears running down my face for the gift he'd just given me. What he'd said to me was, "I trust you, Mom. You are my safe place."

That's the way it should be for children. For God's children too. But can we trust that God wants to cover our shame, our pain? When you believe that your mom or dad will cover you, then it's easier, more natural, to believe that God will cover you too. But when you believe that your parents can't or won't, you learn to cover yourself. Covering myself worked for me . . . until it didn't anymore. Because when the clods of damp earth hit my mum's casket, I wanted to wail. I felt vulnerable, exposed, and uncovered.

Months after my mum's death, after the horrid trip to the beach, and while I was carrying so much pain, God reminded me of that moment with Christian.

I AM your covering.
I AM your Safe Place.
I AM.
Tell Me everything.

As I began this daily practice of honest, vulnerable truth-telling to God, some things were easier for me to confess. Things like disappointment or sadness felt reasonable and mature. They even felt spiritual. What didn't feel spiritual to me, at first, was all the pent-up anger. I had no idea how to properly express it, and that's because

I'd never let it seep out. I'm very well controlled, and I suppose that's good, at least in part. As a mature believer I should be expected to control my anger, but my self-control was not part of my spiritual maturation process. Instead, it had developed during the years I'd stuffed my anger as a child, when I thought it was dangerous and caused death and disappointed God. I began to understand that there was a little girl inside of me who was furious, and I realized that I'd never spoken up for her. I'd told her to be quiet—we wouldn't want to ruin our witness, after all—and she remained silent, but she wasn't happy about it.

Now I know that much of my lifelong struggle with depression started with stuffed anger. When I pushed valid, appropriate emotions down into the cellar of my soul, I lost part of who I really was. I lost part of my authentic self. And in the moments of inauthenticity, in the burying of my anger, I vented through sarcasm. I tried to dress anger up as humor, but it wasn't ever funny because it wounded others.

My other weapon was withdrawal. If I felt myself getting angry, I'd pull back into my secret room, the place inside where no one else was allowed.

Childhood should be the stage when emotions are given a place to play out, where shame and embarrassment go to God for covering. It's the time when children should be given the opportunity to learn the difference between what's healthy and what's destructive and forges isolation. I never learned that, not really. So where do adults go to express emotions that have been buried for so long that they don't even feel as if they belong in their story anymore? It's possible to so detach from that pain that when you try to dig it up it feels inauthentic, like reading the script of someone else's story.

I've watched that healthy process in my son's life. Christian was very close to William, his papa, who lived with us for the last two years of his life. When he died, Christian was overwhelmed with sadness. He cried for days. Then I watched that grief morph into anger one day. He pushed our cat, his beloved playmate Lily, off the sofa. So I asked him to go for a walk with me.

Outside, we strolled side by side toward to the lake. After a while, I asked him to sit down beside me. Then I asked him if he was angry, and he said yes. When I asked why, he said, "You told me that God answers prayers, and I prayed that God wouldn't take my papa, but He did. So I'm not talking to Him anymore."

It was then that I told my son what I wished someone had told me when I was a child.

It's okay to be angry.

It's right to be angry. God is big enough and loves you enough to handle everything you're feeling. I put my arm around Christian's shoulder.

Tell Him everything. He won't leave you.

Soon after that, I bought Christian boxing gloves and a punching bag and told him to hit that thing until he had nothing left.

He also had an almost life-size stuffed lion that we'd bought when he was a little boy, so I told him, "Christian, when you have poured out everything you're feeling, then you can bury your face in the mane of the Lion of Judah."

Great advice. Yet I had no idea how to appropriate it for myself. How often I've stood on stage and encouraged others to be brave and true, to pour out the contents of their hearts to their Father, and yet I was so out of touch with my own feelings. I had no idea how much I needed to do the same.

As I had done many times in the past, I turned to David for help. The authentic cries of a shepherd boy helped me begin to give words to what was locked inside.

"Hear me, LORD, and have mercy on me. Help me, O LORD" (Ps. 30:10).

There was something so intimate about David's words.

"Help me, Lord," he prayed. And it was those three little words that became my prayer. On my knees with my hands open and empty, I felt the anger rise. I didn't explain it away. I just prayed.

"Help me, Lord."

My need didn't leave me alone. My need drew me close.

Confession is now a daily practice for me. Each morning I begin my day with gratitude, thanking God for His love that welcomes me to come as I am. Then I confess what I know to be true no matter what might feel true. I don't always feel loved, but I know I am loved. I don't always feel God's presence, but I know He is with me. I confess my weakness and my fear. I bring everything I know to be true about me into the open arms of Father God.

On this journey I developed such a hunger to return to the stories I'd known since childhood. I read them again, but with fresh eyes and unstopped ears. And in those earliest days of confession, I sat with a man named Job for a long time. Job was a hero of the faith, the kind of man you'd want your daughter to marry. "He was blameless—a man of complete integrity. He feared God and stayed away from evil" (Job 1:1).

Despite that, God allowed Satan to ruin Job's life. His suffering was devastating. He lost everything. He lost his children, his livelihood, and finally his health. His acute suffering took him to the very edge of sanity. His depression spun so black that he prayed: "Obliterate the day I was born. Blank out the night I was conceived! Let it be a black hole in space. May God above forget it ever happened. Erase it from the books! May the day of my birth be buried in deep darkness, shrouded by the fog, swallowed by the night" (Job 3:3–5 MSG).

As his story grew worse and worse, I found myself praying, *God, send this poor man some help! Let his friends gather around him and carry him because he can't even stand anymore.*

Then you meet his friends, who might remind me of some of the Facebook commenters. Eliphaz the Temanite looks at Job and says, "Stop and think! Do the innocent die? When have the upright been destroyed?" (Job 4:7). In other words, "You brought this on yourself, Job." Eliphaz's logic reads something like this: God is good; you are suffering; therefore, you must have done something wrong. It was a theology that left no room for mystery. Instead, this kind of theology is punishing.

Next comes Job's friend Bildad the Shuhite. Knowing Job's children have all been killed in a tragic accident, he brings this attempt at comfort: "Does God twist justice? Does the Almighty twist what is right? Your children must have sinned against him, so their punishment was well deserved" (Job 8:3–4). These words are the ancient equivalent of telling parents who just lost their children in a car wreck, "Well, they shouldn't have been drinking." Perhaps it is true, but that doesn't make it any less cruel.

The words from Job's third friend are no kinder. Zophar says, "Don't you realize that from the beginning of time, ever since people were first placed on the earth, the triumph of the wicked has been short lived . . . ?" (Job 20:4–5). The implication? Job's family, and Job himself, must have been wicked.

As I read through his story, I was furious with these self-righteous friends whose words were many and whose comfort was nonexistent. They felt compelled to explain God and suffering and pain and tie everything up with a nice little faith-bow. And even as I read the story, even as the anger rose, I wondered how many times in the past I've done the same thing. How many times have I slapped a scriptural Band-Aid on an open wound?

Job's friends determine that if he is suffering, it must have been caused by something he's done, something his children have done, or some hidden sin in his past. Back and forth they argue with this devastated man. Job cries out against God: "For he attacks me with a storm and repeatedly wounds me without cause. He will not let me catch my breath, but fills me instead with bitter sorrows" (Job 9:17–18).

The last few chapters of the book of Job are staggering. Job is gut-level honest with God. Job expresses rage and terror peppered by brief moments of faith and hope, and do you know how God responds to that authentic confession? By giving Job His very presence. God reveals Himself to Job.

God doesn't actually answer any of Job's questions. Instead, He gives him a gift far more precious than answers. He gives Job Himself. He pulls back the curtain and shows Job there's a lot more going on than he could even begin to wrap his mind or heart around. God reveals Himself in greater depth and gives Job His presence.

Was God offended by the raw outpouring of a broken heart? Far from it. The only ones God was angry with were the friends who tried to shut him up. Scripture records: "After the LORD had finished speaking to Job, he said to Eliphaz the Temanite: 'I am angry with you and your two friends, for you have not spoken accurately about me, as my servant Job has'" (Job 42:7).

That's a game-changer right there: *for you have not spoken accurately about me, as my servant Job has.* Job was furious. He was bitter, he was broken, he hated his life, he prayed to die, and the raw, authentic bile that poured out of his soul invited the very presence of God. Job spoke truth: "Is not all human life a struggle?" (Job 7:1). In fact, every time Job spoke up, his friends tried to silence him, but he cried out even louder. And it was that truth that invited the love and presence of a tender God.

There is something so important here: Raw, honest pain offered to God brings us closer to His heart. God received everything Job said. He welcomed the brutal, real agony of one who believed God was big enough to hear him out and not silence him into shame and hiding.

---

*Raw, honest pain offered to God
brings us closer to His heart.*

This truth—speaking our honest and raw pain—draws God's presence. We can see this in the life of Jesus too.

Mark's gospel has a definite rhythm to it. If you read it straight through, you can feel the pace picking up as Christ finally sets His face toward Jerusalem and the cross. There is a clock ticking. On the way to Calvary, Jesus tries once more to prepare His closest friends for what is ahead.

"Listen," He says, "we're going up to Jerusalem, where the Son of Man will be betrayed to the leading priests and the teachers of religious law. They will sentence him to die and hand him over to the Romans" (Mark 10:33). Focused, Jesus braces for the betrayal and agony that lies ahead, but suddenly there is a cry that penetrates the noisy crowd. It rises from a blind beggar named Bartimaeus: "Jesus, Son of David, have mercy on me!" (v. 47).

"Be quiet!" many of the people yell.

But he only shouts louder; "Son of David, have mercy on me!" (v. 48).

When Jesus hears Bartimaeus, He stops. Ignoring those who told the poor beggar to stop crying out to the Son of God, Jesus instructs Bartimaeus to come to Him.

"What do you want me to do for you?" Jesus asks (v. 51).

Bartimaeus responds, "I want to see."

And Jesus responds by healing Bartimaeus.

I love the way my friend Lisa Harper expresses the truth of this story: "Jesus paused Easter to listen to one man." He was on His way to the cross, to the grave, to the resurrection, but He stopped for one.

Bartimaeus followed Jesus after that. He was at the cross. He was there after the resurrection. Church history tells us he became part of the early church. His relationship began by crying out his need, even when everyone around him told him to be quiet.

Friends of mine have tried to silence me the way the people of Jesus' day tried to silence Bartimaeus. Well-meaning folks have cautioned me: "Don't ever tell people that you were in a mental hospital. It'll ruin your ministry." But I knew the truth and grew braver about proclaiming it over the years. "I'm not trying to save my ministry," I'd say. "I'm trying to save my life."

When people have told me that there's no reason to be angry because joy comes in the morning, I've told them that it's still the night, that I still need to sit in my anger and to ask Christ to visit me there and heal me from it. This is what it means for me to live a truthful, authentic life. Through the years I've found that God always meets me in my authenticity. Every time. Without fail.

How do you live an authentic life with God? It always starts with the truth. Telling the truth to Christ saves us, right there in the middle of our mess. It exposes who we really are and allows our authentic selves—our darkest secrets, shames, and shadows—to be redeemed. Tell Him the truth. Pour out your pain like Job. Call out to Him like Bartimaeus. Tell Him the whole truth as best you know it, regardless of what your friends or the crowd might say. That's what I'm learning to do, and it's changing my life. This crying out is bringing me healing and strength amid my brokenness. It's bringing me into the realization of the truth—that Christ longs to love every part of me, even my ragged, raw, and emotional parts.

If you still have one breath and there's not a white chalk mark around your body, it's not too late to begin living and loving differently, authentically. Bartimaeus's name meant "the blind one." Meeting Jesus changed his very identity. It will change how we see ourselves too.

As I walk in honest confession, I find that I'm no longer the keep-it-together or stuff-the-emotions girl. Instead, I am a well-loved daughter, even when my emotions aren't the picture of Christian perfection. And that's who you are too—well loved. Don't hide your pain. God welcomes you as you are. Cry out. The depth of your honesty invites the glory of God's presence.

The depth of your

honesty

invites the

glory

of God's presence.

Reflection

The daily confession of sin is a powerful tool of healing and deliverance.

I don't know your suffering. I don't know your need. But I wonder if—for a moment—you can sit in the quiet of Christ's presence as He looks at you with eyes of pure love. Do you hear Him asking you, "What do you want Me to do for you?" That's what I've learned to do.

Can you cry out to Him? Can you pour out all your frustration and anger and need, and still trust that He'll meet you there? What's more, can you pour out your questions, pour out the whole truth even in the presence of your friends, trusting that God will show you His faithful love?

> Even though I walk through the valley
>   of the shadow of death,
> I will fear no evil,
> for you are with me;
> your rod and your staff,
> they comfort me.
>
> —Psalm 23:4 ESV

Chapter 6

❧

Let Go

*What comes into our minds when we think about
God is the most important thing about us.*

—A. W. TOZER

O ne of the gifts of pouring out what I'd held inside for so long is
that it made space for the new. As I began a daily, sometimes
hourly practice of confessing my feelings, my sin, my fear, and my
anger to God, I realized that it created inside of me a wide-open
space for grace. Not only grace but quiet. I used to be afraid of quiet,
afraid I'd hear the dogs of war barking in the cellar of my soul. Now
I love it. I love to sit quietly with the Lord. If the Holy Spirit brings
something to mind that I need to offer up to God, I do. I'm no longer
afraid of being exposed because I know I am loved.

In the morning when I first wake up, I love to meditate on this
verse: "Be still, and know that I am God" (Ps. 46:10). It's the first verse
I learned as a child from my mother. It was the first verse she learned
from her godly grandmother. She told me that Psalm 46 had been a
source of strength to Scottish women through two World Wars. During
World War I, in particular, when men from the Highlands and Islands

were called up to fight, they would gather on the pier waiting for transportation over to the mainland, and together with their loved ones, they would sing this hymn from the Church of Scotland Hymnbook:

> God is our refuge and our strength,
>   in straits a present aid;
> Therefore, although the earth remove,
>   we will not be afraid:
>
> Though hills amidst the seas be cast;
>   Though waters roaring make,
> And troubled be; yea, though the hills
>   by swelling seas do shake.
>
> A river is, whose streams do glad
>   the city of our God;
> The holy place, wherein the Lord
>   most high hath his abode.
>
> God in the midst of her doth dwell;
>   nothing shall her remove:
> The Lord to her a helper will,
>   and that right early prove.
>
> Be still and know that I am God:
>   among the heathen I
> Will be exalted; I on earth
>   will be exalted high.
>
> Our God, who is the Lord of hosts,
>   is still upon our side:
> The God of Jacob our refuge
>   for ever will abide.

Through the years, I've learned to dig deeper into the Word of God and gain greater understanding of the original meaning of the text that we sometimes miss. One that still stands out to me is that verse from the Psalms: "Be still and know that I am God" (46:10).

The Hebrew root of the words *be still* means "to release, go slack, to let go." And when I contemplate that truth, somehow I understand it more. As a child I would try and sit and just be quiet, but this verse has become part of my daily spiritual practice.

Let go and know that I am God.

Let go of what you're trying to fix. Let go of trying to be in control. Let go of the things you don't like about yourself. Let go of your expectations of the day ahead. Let go; let go; let go. Let go and know that He is God.

With this as an intentional, daily practice to begin my day, I can even let go of the hardest thoughts I've ever buried inside. Such as, *Some days I don't want to be here.*

That's hard to say out loud. It sounds shocking even to my ears. It feels weak and unfaithful. I love Christ. I have no life, no future, no hope without Him, but even still, there are days when I find the struggle with depression and suicidal thoughts a hard climb. My years of saying what I thought was *the right thing* or *the proper Christian thing* make it more of a struggle to let go of my pride and say *the real thing* in any given moment.

But I know now that if I don't speak out the raw questions and emotions, if I don't cry out like Job or Bartimaeus, I don't invite the presence of God into my pain. If I don't speak the truth, the emotions lurk beneath the surface, weakening my spiritual legs. They stay deep down inside, waiting for the next emotional storm to wash them back up to the shoreline of my soul. In the practice of confession, of letting go in the quiet of my morning routine, here's what I've found: the words that seem hard to say lose their power when I speak them aloud because they are exposed to the power of Christ.

I think back to some of my darkest moments. There were nights when I was awake and alone and would begin thinking about a bottle of pills in my medicine cabinet, how swallowing the entire batch would be a quick and easy way to be free of my struggle. I never said it out loud because I thought it would make it more real or somehow give power to those shadow thoughts, but that's not true. Instead, I've learned that saying the darkest things I've felt, bringing my whole self into His light, brings peace.

In His light, I feel His love and comfort. And grasping the truth that I'm not "less than" in the eyes of Jesus when I pour out my heart has made His presence even sweeter. It's made my life feel secure and held. That's why I confess my darkness to Him daily. That's why I sit in the stillness and meditate on how He loves me despite my darkness—every day.

I spend a great deal of my time teaching at women's conferences, large and small. And as much as I love teaching, I learn as much from the women I teach as they do from me. Hearing from others how their faith is challenged and changed opens me up to the amazing things that Christ is doing in and through His church body. In this kind of give-and-take community, we grow together.

I can tell when something I'm talking about connects with an audience or needs further exploration. When it seems I've only scratched the surface of what the audience is dealing with, we dig deeper—at least, in theory. I've discovered that not everyone will celebrate your freedom. There will be those who don't understand or won't be comfortable when you begin telling the truth. In those moments, letting go becomes even more important.

Last year I was speaking to a small group of women in Texas. We were looking at how Christ helps us in moments when it appears that heaven is silent, when prayers are not given an answer that makes sense to us. I told them that I still deal with depression but have learned to invite Christ into that place. I asked them to take that to a broader, more personal room in their own lives. I gave a few suggestions.

You might be struggling in your marriage.
You may be having a difficult time with a child who's rejecting everything that you've taught them.
Perhaps you're struggling with a coworker.
You may be wrestling with your own self-image.

My basic premise was that whatever is difficult at the moment, whatever emotions you may feel as a result of that difficulty, Jesus wants to be in it with you. No matter how overwhelming or how seemingly small, Christ wants you to call out to Him.

After we spent some time reflecting, I asked everyone to take a fifteen-minute break. I was about to head back to the study room I'd been using and make a cup of tea when a woman approached me. She said she needed to talk to me before the final session. I stopped to listen.

"What you just shared was straight from the pit of hell," she began.

I was so shocked that I don't think I replied.

"Don't you know that all diseases, all cancers, all mental illnesses were canceled out at the cross of Christ?" she asked.

I paused for a moment, looking in her eyes. She seemed desperate to communicate her point. Quietly I asked Christ to help me hear her heart more than her words.

No words came—at least not immediately. I stood, blinking for a few moments and then said, "I believe with all my heart that Christ is more than able to heal every bit of human suffering, but there are times when He doesn't this side of eternity. Then we need His grace and presence even more."

"That's a *lie!*" she said. "It's a lie and a sin."

I'll spare you the rest, as it got worse. I had to ask her if I could excuse myself before the next session began. I went into my room and closed the door. I felt like a five-year-old who had just been disciplined for being a bad girl. I shut the door to the noise outside and sat on the floor of the pastor's study. In the quiet, I talked to Jesus.

What was that? Why would she do that? Why would she even come to a conference like this if that's what she believes?

I was hurt and I was mad, and her scolding had opened old wounds. A part of me still wanted to tell her to go home and take her ugly heart with her. But I sat there with God. And I confessed my feelings to my Father.

Let go and know that I am God. Release these things and know that I am God.

I let the love and mercy of Christ seep into those old places of misunderstanding or rejection. And as I sat in the quiet stillness of His love, Christ gave me the eyes to see that woman as someone who probably had been as hurt and broken in her past as I had been. I sat there and lifted her up to Christ, asking that He would flood every place in her heart with love, mercy, and grace.

I tried to find her when the conference was over, but she was gone. So, too, were my feelings of having been wronged or misunderstood.

When I stop reacting from a place of pain and instead respond by taking my wounds to God, I find peace. By meditating on His great love for me, even in the middle of my messy emotions, I find strength.

Only then can I understand that I am a well-loved child of God. Only then can I respond from a place of love.

Part of my journey to a deeper, more intimate relationship with Christ has been learning to tell Him the whole truth, each and every day. I long for you to join me in this practice. Not only does it lighten the load we carry, but also it becomes a minute-by-minute understanding of the beautiful companionship we are invited to share with Christ. Telling Him the whole truth is the antidote to loneliness.

When I stop

reacting

from a place of

pain and instead

respond

by taking my

wounds to God, I

find *peace.*

For years I've kept a journal beside my Bible so that I may write down anything that I feel the Holy Spirit is saying about the text that day. Recently I looked at things I'd written in the past, and it was eye-opening. I was as truthful as I knew how to be when I wrote those words, but I question some of those insights now. Being raised in an extremely conservative church since I was a child, my knee-jerk response to most of life was to say *the right thing,* whether or not it felt true at the moment.

In one entry from my thirties, I wrote, "Even if I find myself in a very dark place I know that God is with me." But I know now that when I found myself in a very dark place back then, I wasn't sure where God was. It's only when I am able to be honest with God—telling Him that I'm not sure He was with me as I stood on the edge of the bridge or sat with a bottle of pills in my hand—that I am able to receive the beautiful news that He *was* right there, with me, all along. He never left my side. The worse I reveal about myself, the greater the revelation of His presence.

My doubts and questions didn't push Him away; instead, He drew closer. So close, in fact, that I finally began to understand that He is my Safe Place who has been there all along. Even when I felt desperate and alone, He was with me. When I thought the darkness would swallow me whole, He was there. No matter how deep the waters, how blinding the pain, how silent the grave, no matter what, God was there. And He wasn't there in a metaphorical sense. He was as close to me as my next breath.

David knew this same truth. He welcomed it into his darkest moments. He had committed adultery and arranged the death of one of his most faithful men. David's intentional sins wounded many. Even though he was one who failed miserably, it comforted him to know that the only One who knew everything about him was God. In Psalm 139, he wrote it this way:

> O LORD, you have examined my heart
> and know everything about me.

You know when I sit down or stand up.

  You know my thoughts even when I'm far away.

You see me when I travel

  and when I rest at home.

  You know everything I do.

You know what I am going to say

  even before I say it, LORD.

You go before me and follow me.

  You place your hand of blessing on my head.

Such knowledge is too wonderful for me,

  too great for me to understand!

I can never escape from your Spirit!

  I can never get away from your presence!

If I go up to heaven, you are there;

  if I go down to the grave, you are there.

If I ride the wings of the morning,

  if I dwell by the farthest oceans,

even there your hand will guide me,

  and your strength will support me.

I could ask the darkness to hide me

  and the light around me to become night—

  but even in darkness I cannot hide from you.

To you the night shines as bright as day.

  Darkness and light are the same to you. (vv. 1–12)

David knew that no matter what he did, he couldn't shake the presence of God. And that knowledge filled him with praise.

What I believe about God has changed over time. I used to believe that God was disappointed in me if I failed or gave into despair. Equally wrong, I believed at times that God approved of me because of good choices I made. But none of that is true. The truth is simple, if not difficult to believe: When God looks at me, He sees the finished work of Jesus. He sees me as pure, washed, clean, white—a beautiful, well-loved girl. He sees you that way too. Is that hard to believe about yourself?

Being as honest as you can be, pause for a moment here and ask yourself: "What comes into my mind when I think about God?"

Do you think He's good?
Do you think He's for you?
Do you think He's proud of you?
Do you think He cares about you personally?
Do you think He loves you as much on your worst days as He does when you're in a good place?
Do you think He hears and answers your prayers?

How we answer these questions will determine whether we trust Him with our confession, and whether we will make Him our Safe Place. It will determine whether we'll still worship Him when nothing in our life makes sense, when it seems that the very God who loves us is silent.

Even Christ had to face the silence of God, had to make the decision to tell the whole truth. In an article published by *Christianity Today*, Ziya Meral wrote: "The greatest glory Jesus brought to God was not when he walked on the water or prayed for long hours, but when he cried in agony in the garden of Gethsemane and still continued to follow God's will, even though it meant isolation, darkness, and the silence of God."[1]

Crucifixion was the most despicable way to die in the Roman world. It was barbaric, shameful, and excruciatingly painful. When a condemned criminal was on his way to be crucified, he was made to carry the crossbeam himself. It was clear to everyone watching that this was a one-way ticket. He would not be returning. Yet Christ set His face toward the cross.

Still, do you remember what Jesus told His friends in the Garden of Gethsemane? Do you remember how He prayed? "He told them, 'My soul is crushed with grief to the point of death. Stay here and keep watch with me.' He went on a little farther and bowed with his face to the ground, praying, 'My Father! If it is possible, let this cup of suffering be taken away from me. Yet I want your will to be done, not mine'" (Matt. 26:38–39).

Jesus didn't pretend that He gladly embraced the agony of crucifixion. He didn't spin some syrupy theological truth about the glory of suffering. Instead, He told the truth—first to His friends, then in the stillness of His Father's presence. He was deeply troubled, distressed, anxious, and devastated, and that's how He prayed. If Jesus didn't think that being honest showed a lack of faith, why should we? The good news of salvation is that you get to be honest; you don't have to bury your emotions. Christianity is not a place to hide; it's a place to come into the fullness of light. It's a place to come into the daily safety of Christ's presence.

The good news of salvation is that you get to be honest; you don't have to bury your emotions.

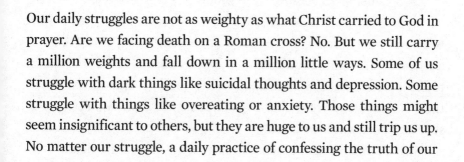

Our daily struggles are not as weighty as what Christ carried to God in prayer. Are we facing death on a Roman cross? No. But we still carry a million weights and fall down in a million little ways. Some of us struggle with dark things like suicidal thoughts and depression. Some struggle with things like overeating or anxiety. Those things might seem insignificant to others, but they are huge to us and still trip us up. No matter our struggle, a daily practice of confessing the truth of our emotions to Christ—even the hardest truths—helps so much. Through this daily confession, we come into the realization of how much God loves us. We have the privilege of sitting in that love, of meditating on it.

"Meditating?" you might ask. Yes, meditating.

Perhaps you were raised in a tradition where meditation wasn't part of the spiritual disciplines. That was true for me. But this is what I've discovered: If you know how to worry, if you know how to stuff away your feelings and obsess over them, then you know how to meditate. Instead, you can recognize the worry, confess it, release it to God, and change what it is you're thinking about. You do this day in and day out, letting go, and letting go, and letting go. In time, the practice of letting go, of recognizing God's love, becomes second nature. It becomes your meditation.

David wrote, "I lie awake thinking of you, meditating on you through the night" (Ps. 63:6). The Hebrew word for *meditate* here is *hagah*. It means "to mutter or to coo like a dove." I don't know if you've ever listened to a dove's cooing. Such a lovely persistent sound. The idea here is to keep turning the words of Scripture over and over in our minds until the truth sinks from our heads to the deepest places in our spirits.

Be still and know that I am God. Let go. This is an invitation to you.

Reflection

Meditation is a lost discipline in much of the evangelical church. One of the key differences between biblical meditation and Eastern or transcendental meditation is that the latter tells its followers to empty their minds. Christian meditation encourages us to fill our minds with the Word and the presence of God. We are not called to "find ourselves" but rather to find ourselves in Him. We are not called to "go on a journey" but rather to follow the way of the cross.

So, where to begin?

Just start. This is not an exercise for a select few believers who are perceived to be spiritually mature. Meditation is an open gate to living in the mercy and presence of God for all who will come.

Let me suggest a few verses to help you begin. If you can, commit the texts to memory. If not, write them on a card and keep them with you. Use whatever translation you prefer. Take time each morning to be quiet and prepare your heart to meditate on a text. Ask yourself: "How does this verse speak into my life? What does it say about God? What does it say about me?" Then ask God to make His Word alive and active in your life.

> I will meditate on your majestic, glorious splendor
> and your wonderful miracles.
>
> —Psalm 145:5

> You will keep in perfect peace
> all who trust in you,
> all whose thoughts are fixed on you!
>
> —Isaiah 26:3

> So now there is no condemnation for
>   those who belong to Christ Jesus.
>
> —Romans 8:1

> The LORD is my shepherd;
> I have all that I need.
>
> —Psalm 23:1

Chapter 7

Beautifully Broken

He had never known before, the strength of the want in
his heart for the frequent recognition of a nod, a look,
a word; or the immense amount of relief that had been
poured into it by drops, through such small means.

—CHARLES DICKENS, *HARD TIMES*

As summer gave way to the early days of fall, I felt ready to take another look at my mother's things. Most of them were still in my backpack, which I'd placed in my closet after my return from Scotland.

It had taken us some time to sort through Mum's estate. My sister Frances, my sister-in-law Mary, and I had gone through Mum's jewelry, choosing pieces that had special meaning to us. I was supposed to get Mum's engagement ring, but it was missing. In the last few years of her life, Mum had lost her attachments to many of her possessions. She also forgot that a few of them were valuable. I imagined that she exchanged the ring with one of the other residents for a box of chocolates, or a plant, or some other little Airlie House treasure. I imagined that the exchange brought her a moment of joy, and if that were the case, I was happy for her.

Mum had wanted Frances to have her gold watch. Mary took the long strand of pearls. I took her silver locket and the shorter strand of pearls she wore on her wedding day. The locket contains a photograph of Mum on one side and Dad on the other. Dad is wearing a plain white shirt, collar open at the neck. His hair is dark, and he is smiling and handsome. Mum is dressed in a floral dress, and her long dark hair is blowing in the wind. They look so young and full of life. I wish I could have known them then.

We found her ration book from World War II, her first Bible, and letters from her closest friends she had kept after my father's death. I left most of the papers with Frances but took a few with me, including one or two that Mum had written. I've always loved her penmanship. She wrote beautifully. Her cursive handwriting was small, but each word was perfectly spaced—such a lost art.

When we'd been through everything, I carefully placed the chosen treasures from my mum's life into my backpack and flew back to Dallas. Back at home, I only took out her *Yes, Lord!* picture and her stuffed rabbit. I left everything else in the bag that now sat in the back of my closet.

One afternoon Barry had a doctor's appointment and the dogs were at the groomer's, so the house was unusually quiet. I walked to my closet, retrieved the backpack, and brought it downstairs. I made myself a cup of tea and sat down at our dining-room table with the backpack next to me. I took a deep breath and reached inside. The first thing I pulled out was the Bible Mum had received in 1939. It was given as the first prize in a competition for the best pressed flowers. The flowers were still there, carefully kept inside the front cover—Scottish bluebells. I imagined her as a little girl bending down in a summer dress, carefully selecting each of these vibrant lilac-blue flowers that carpet much of Scotland in the summer months.

Next, I pulled out a worn little cardboard box. Inside were all her badges from Junior Christian Endeavor, a nondenominational movement for young people Mum had joined in her teens. In my teens, I followed suit. Our motto was: "For Christ and the Church." She had kept her pledge card, and she'd kept mine too. It made me smile. I remember every Thursday night standing with my friends in the upstairs room at Ayr Baptist Church reciting our pledge.

> Trusting in the Lord Jesus Christ for strength, I promise Him that I will strive to do whatever He would like to have me do; that I will make it the rule of my life to pray and to read the Bible every day, and to support the work and worship of my own church in every way possible; and that just so far as I know how, throughout my whole life, I will endeavor to lead a Christian life.
>
> As an active member I promise to be true to all my duties, to be present at and to take some part, in every Christian Endeavor meeting.

I placed the Bible and the cards to the side and pulled out a folder with "Airlie House" written on the front. Inside were some reports on Mum's health, including a few recommendations from a social worker encouraging her to get a little exercise. At the back of a folder was a fill-in-the-blank form where Mum had scribbled some answers.

The first query read, "Things you would like to do more of," and Mum had written, "International travel." I grinned and laughed out loud. It was hard for her to make it from her room to the dining hall in those last days, but in her spirit she hadn't changed a bit. She'd always loved to travel.

Next she'd written, "I'd like to Skype with my daughter in America." Tears welled up as I remembered the time we'd tried it, the time she looked into the computer and declared, "If I knew I was going to be on television, I'd have combed my hair." That attempt at Skype had been a bit of a disaster, but her words expressed how much she wanted connection with me, how often she thought of me.

She remembered where I lived and she wanted to see my face. I'll treasure that piece of paper forever.

"Tell us some things about yourself," the form said next. Mum had written, "I like to ride bikes." That was true. She was an avid cyclist in her teens and twenties, and when I was a girl, she and I would take long bike rides out into the countryside. We'd stop after a while, find a quiet spot, and sit on a blanket eating tomato sandwiches, trying to identify all the wildflowers around us.

She next wrote, "I like spicy food. It's a bit bland here," which was a surprise to me. She'd never been a fan of spicy foods, at least not as far as I knew. Of course, I suppose our tastes change as we age.

Lastly, she wrote, "I am a good friend." I felt my stomach shift, and the tears welled. My mum was able to see the truth about herself. I believe my mum had worked through the dark moments of her life, through shame and lies, and had been able to recognize her own beauty. My mum had left me more that I initially realized.

For so many reasons, I've had difficulty making definitive, positive statements about myself. I instinctively deflect compliments. I thought back to the day when we were cleaning out her room at Airlie. Margaret Rankin, Mum's friend since childhood, popped her head around the door to see if we needed any old newspapers to wrap things in. I gratefully accepted and followed her back to her room. She gave me the papers, then took my hand and said, "Your mum was a good friend to me."

I thought about Maureen Martin, Mum's closest friend, who was killed in a head-on collision with a truck when I was in my twenties. A small framed picture of her always sat beside Mum's fireside chair. I dug deeper into my backpack and found the old photo of Maureen. I was so glad to have it. I loved her too.

I remembered the nights when either Margaret or Maureen came over to be with Mum after we'd gone to bed. She saw them every week, and they often talked deep into the night. Every Christmas Eve, a big box would arrive on our doorstep with a turkey and all the trimmings from Maureen and her husband, Jim. When Margaret's husband, Robert, passed away, Mum spent a lot of time with her. Last Christmas, I pulled a little hedgehog ornament from the hamper marked "special ornaments." It had been a gift from Margaret one year when I'd taken a quick trip home to Scotland with Christian. Mum had said, "Let's take Margaret out for lunch," and when we said good-bye, Margaret handed me that little hedgehog and said, "For your tree. Remember all the good times."

"I am a good friend," my mum had written. It was so true. Her friends were good too.

I had wanted to be able to share Mum's darkest moments and know what she felt. I didn't want her to cry alone, but looking at the photo of Maureen, I began to see that she really hadn't been alone. She'd allowed her closest friends into that sacred space where her truest self lived. Mum had her community, a safe group of sisters to whom she could confess those things most people hide from even God. They were her sisters of confession and prayer, and they made a place where grief and joy, hopes and dreams, darkness and light could be shared.

As a child I'd built a walled-off hiding place that was intended to protect me from being hurt by others. I thought she had too. Looking back now, though, I don't think that was true. Mum knew she needed more than confession to her heavenly Father. She needed a safe community where she could be vulnerable, a community that would love her amid her vulnerability. She found it in her community of sisters. And through walking with those sisters, I think Mum discovered the secret to the depth of salvation, to bringing her most authentic self to Christ. She wasn't a woman marked by her pain. She was intimately known and accepted. She was well loved.

⸙

Confessing the darkness to God, letting go and allowing Him to speak love to us is imperative if we want to find strength in the

middle of our messy lives. But without genuine community, community where we are known, loved, and received, it's hard to push past
the lies that haunt us. I've tried to find spiritual growth by myself,
without others, and it didn't work. In the weeks and months before
I had my first breakdown in 1992, I'd done everything I knew to
get closer to God. I read my Bible and I prayed, but I felt so frozen.
In a final desperate attempt to thaw, to uncover any hidden sin or
disobedience that caused my hopelessness, I fasted and prayed for
twenty-one days. The result wasn't a great spiritual breakthrough;
instead, I became a patient in a psychiatric ward.

---

*Confessing the darkness to God, letting
go and allowing Him to speak love to us
is imperative if we want to find strength
in the middle of our messy lives.*

In retrospect, that stay in the hospital provided the catalyst for
the spiritual breakthrough I longed for. Sometimes God's greatest
gifts make our hands bleed, but they are His greatest gifts nonethe-
less. It was in this community of the mentally ill that I first began
to experience what it's like to let someone into the hidden places, to
share your secrets and expose the stuff kept behind the wall.

Each day I'd sit in a circle with other patients and introduce
myself when it was my turn. I didn't understand what we were
doing at first—or why.

"I'm Michael, and I'm here because I tried to kill myself," a man
with scarred wrists said.

"I'm Susan, and I'm here because I'm anorexic," a gaunt woman
with stringy blonde hair said.

"I'm Sheila, and I have no idea why I'm here."

I didn't like our group meetings at first. Some days I felt threatened by their terrifying authenticity and vulnerability, but mostly I was scared by their questions.

"Why do you hold yourself back from us?"

"Why are you afraid to say what's true for you?"

"When you're ready to fall off your shelf, Sheila, we'll be here."

The thought of opening the cellar door of my soul was too much. I'd believed all my life that if I let anyone else see the worst parts, I'd be left utterly alone. But the sad truth is, holding back my true self made me alone. By isolating those parts of myself, I was never really known by anyone.

I remember the day when I couldn't stay quiet anymore. The room was silent. It was my turn to say something. Everyone else had bared their souls for days, inviting Christ and one another into their pain. They were tired of my polite, contained responses, so they waited for me to speak. I honestly don't remember my exact words, but I remember it felt like a house falling down inside me, like a massive tornado destroying my walls. I finally fell off my shelf.

I told them that I hated myself.

I told them that I wish I'd died and my dad had lived.

I told them I was living on borrowed or stolen time, and I wished it was over.

I told them I was so afraid and so alone.

That's when something holy happened. As I fell to my knees on the worn, blue carpet of our group-therapy room, tears streaming down my cheeks, they gathered around me, holding me, praying out loud for me. I felt as if I had been carried to the foot of the cross. I'd never felt so naked yet so covered, so vulnerable but so safe. Scriptures I had poured over the wounds of others now began to pour over me.

"You keep track of all my sorrows. You have collected all my tears in your bottle. You have recorded each one in your book" (Ps. 56:8).

"He comforts us in all our troubles so that we can comfort others. When they are troubled, we will be able to give them the same comfort God has given us" (2 Cor. 1:4).

After our session that day, I went out into the patients' prayer garden. I sat on the bench beside the fountain, listening to the water tumbling over stones. I was raw and exhausted, but I felt the love of God through the outpouring of that community. I didn't have words to pray, but I didn't need any. The presence of Christ was with me.

It's a battle to drag the secrets and lies we've believed about ourselves into the light, but it's there that we find hope and healing. That doesn't happen on our own. It only happens when we invite trusted sisters into our secrets.

The Scriptures say, "Confess your sins to each other and pray for each other so that you may be healed" (James 5:16). I've found this to be true. We all need community to help us carry our load, to walk with us through the pain, to carry us to our resurrection experience.

You may be tempted to dismiss this need for community as pop-psychology. Shouldn't God be enough for us? Isn't He sufficient? But do you remember how Christ modeled community for us? Do you remember how He craved the intimacy of others?

Jesus was intentional about the community He chose, the twelve men who became His disciples. Yes, men had been following Him for about a year into His ministry, but when it was time to choose the ones to whom He'd entrust His teaching, He first spent the night alone with God in prayer. Luke records it this way: "One day soon afterward Jesus went up on a mountain to pray, and he prayed to God all night. At daybreak he called together all of his disciples and chose twelve of them to be apostles" (Luke 6:12–13).

What did He see in these men? They were far from perfect. Most of them were very rough around the edges. But Christ must have known that when everything they believed to be true about themselves crashed and burned, they would find their identity in Him and His mission. And He knew, too, that in this close-knit community, He'd find a band of friends. It was with these friends, this community of the twelve, that He shared the glories and tragedies of His ministry.

Even still, when it came time for Jesus to experience the heights or the depths, He narrowed His community to His three closest friends—Peter, James, and John. They were the ones present at the transfiguration. The Scriptures teach:

> About eight days later Jesus took Peter, John, and James up on a mountain to pray. And as he was praying, the appearance of his face was transformed, and his clothes became dazzling white. Suddenly, two men, Moses and Elijah, appeared and began talking with Jesus. They were glorious to see. And they were speaking about his exodus from this world, which was about to be fulfilled in Jerusalem. Peter and the others had fallen asleep. When they woke up, they saw Jesus' glory and the two men standing with him. As Moses and Elijah were starting to leave, Peter, not even knowing what he was saying, blurted out, "Master, it's wonderful for us to be here! Let's make three shelters as memorials—one for you, one for Moses, and one for Elijah." But even as he was saying this, a cloud overshadowed them, and terror gripped them as the cloud covered them. Then a voice from the cloud said, "This is my Son, my Chosen One. Listen to him." (Luke 9:28–35)

This encounter was the pinnacle of Christ's earthly ministry, and though we don't know what was said on that mountainside, it's clear that Peter, John, and James saw Christ at His most glorious moment.

Those friends were invited to follow Him into the depths of suffering too. The night before His crucifixion, they followed Him to another mountain, the mountain of His suffering. They entered the

Garden of Gethsemane with Him: "Then Jesus went with them to the olive grove called Gethsemane, and he said, 'Sit here while I go over there to pray.' He took Peter and Zebedee's two sons, James and John, and he became anguished and distressed. He told them, 'My soul is crushed with grief to the point of death. Stay here and keep watch with me'" (Matt. 26:36–38).

Christ was fully God but fully man. It's a mystery too great for us to understand, but in these final hours of His life Jesus needed His closest friends. He left the other eight disciples (Judas had already left to betray Christ) at the entrance of the Garden, but He invited Peter, James, and John to follow Him in. Christ, the God-man, was about to take the weight of the world's sin on His shoulders; He was about to carry the secrets and shame of all mankind to the death. And feeling the weight of that sin and shame, He invited His three closest friends into His grief.

Stay here and keep watch with Me.

Stay with Me.

Christmas will come again and again, and when the season begins this year, I'll start by pulling the tree from the attic. I'll pull out my "special ornaments" hamper and enjoy the ones Christian made when he was a child. There are the snowflakes we cut out when he was four years old and covered with glitter and glue, more glue than glitter. There is the first manger ornament he crafted at school where Christ is an alarmingly gigantic baby. We have his photos with Santa framed and ready to hang, and even the ornament he made of Christ on the cross that, at seven, he informed us was the real point of Christmas. We hang that one each year, even though Jesus has only one leg. Christian's simple childhood explanation was: "I ran out of modeling clay. Jesus will understand." Near the bottom of the hamper, I'll find the hedgehog from Margaret. I'll lift it out carefully as I remember Margaret's words: "For your tree. Remember all the good times."

Even as I consider that ornament, I think back to the many times I stood at the front of our home church, as the soloist at our Christmas Eve service. I remember the song I sang, an old hymn for children:

Little children, wake and listen!
Songs are breaking o'er the earth;
While the stars in heaven glisten,
Hear the news of Jesus' birth.
Long ago, to lonely meadows,
Angels brought the message down;
Still, each year, through midnight shadows,
It is heard in every town.

What is this that they are telling,
Singing in the quiet street?
While their voices high are swelling,
What sweet words do they repeat?
Words to bring us greater gladness,
Though our hearts from care are free;
Words to chase away our sadness,
Cheerless though our hearts may be.

Mum, Maureen, and Margaret were always there. I'd look at them if I was nervous, which I always was, and they would smile. Now Maureen and Mum are safely home.

On the day of Mum's funeral, I stepped up to the same pulpit to give the eulogy, and there sat Margaret, smiling up at me. Weak and frail, but faithful to Mum right to the end. She was a safe place for my mum. I believe they let each other into the secret places. They understood the importance of community, of sisters who are always there.

When I reflect on my mother's friends and on the women who are dear to me, I realize that if we are to connect with safe-place sisters, we need humility. In humility, we show up on our best days and our worst.

As women, it's easy to fall into the trap of misunderstanding what that means. It's not inflating ourselves or selling ourselves short; it is radical truth-telling. A. W. Tozer described it like this: "The meek man is not a human mouse afflicted with a sense of his own inferiority. Rather he may be in his moral life as bold as a lion and as strong as Samson; but he has stopped being fooled about himself."[1]

Humility can be tough to grasp. I spent so much of my life deflecting kind words, not taking credit for anything and thinking it was humility. It was the opposite. That kind of "humility" is simply pride in reverse. When we think we're too good or not good enough we've missed what humility is. Rather than a mask to hide behind, humility is an unveiling of who we are.

Humility is a heart thing. It's allowing yourself to be loved as you are and extending that grace to others. My mum's relationships with her friends have blessed me all my life. Their safe community echoed the safety of Christ and reminds me of my need for the same. When my mum died, my own safe-place sisters were there. With them beside me, I faced down the lies that came haunting in the months afterward. Together, we find strength for this beautiful, broken life together. I wish the same for you, a safe community of sisters who come together in humility and lifelong love.

Reflection

We can't live in true community without humility. Humility calls us to live an unpretentious life that makes intimacy, confession, and true sisterhood possible.

The life of Christ is the most radical picture of humility. For God to become a man was humbling enough, but Christ went much further: "Have this mind among yourselves, which is yours in Christ Jesus, who, though he was in the form of God, did not count equality with God a thing to be grasped, but emptied himself, by taking the form of a servant, being born in the likeness of men. And being found in human form, he humbled himself by becoming obedient to the point of death, even death on a cross" (Phil. 2:5–8 ESV).

He could have come as He is—King of kings. Yet He chose to come as a baby and was born into a poor family. He veiled His glory. His path was a continual stepping down. He came as a man, He became a servant, and He died as a common criminal. And while He walked on the earth, He chose to be known. He invited His friends into not only the moments of His glory but also the agony of His suffering. This divine, outrageous courage calls us out of our private places into community. It requires emptying ourselves in raw vulnerability. And that requires humility that can only come from above.

Would you like to have that kind of openness? Do you trust the Lord to lead you to safe-place, sisters? Read the verse below and ask the Lord to show you the joy of sharing your true self with Him and in a community of sisters.

> For the LORD delights in his people;
> he crowns the humble with victory.
>
> —Psalm 149:4

Humility

is a heart thing.

It's allowing

yourself

to be loved as

you are and

extending

that grace to others.

Chapter 8

⤜⤛

Rejecting the Lies We've Believed

When we honestly ask ourselves which persons in our lives mean the most to us, we often find that it is those who, instead of giving much advice, solutions, or cures, have chosen rather to share our pain and touch our wounds with a gentle and tender hand.

—HENRI NOUWEN, *OUT OF SOLITUDE*

Just before Thanksgiving 2013, my friend Lisa Harper and I were invited to the red-carpet premiere of Max Lucado's movie *The Christmas Candle*, which was opening in Dallas.

Lisa flew in from Nashville, and Barry and I picked her up at the airport.

Lisa and I are usually the jeans-and-boots sort of girls, but that night, Lisa wore a black St. John knit suit, and I wore a copper-colored evening dress. Pulling into the parking lot, we could see the camera crew at the end of the red carpet and a Salvation Army band playing by the entrance to the theater.

Barry, as usual, parked as far away as possible from other cars to protect our car from the dings of other car doors. If Barry's driving, I usually wear comfortable shoes for the walk from where we've parked to where we're going. Why he didn't drop us off at the front, I have no idea; instead he found what he thought was the perfect spot beside a large tree. As soon as I stepped out of the car, my five-inch heels sank into wet grass. Barry tried to steady me, but in the process, he only succeeded in pushing me over.

Lisa doubled over, howling, and gingerly made her way to me in the heels she was wearing. She tried to help me up, which caused her heels to sink into the mud too. Then she lost her balance and ended up on her knees beside me. Instead of helping, Barry pulled out his camera and began snapping pictures of us crawling across the wet grass like two covert Navy SEALs in dresses. When she collapsed into laughter, I did too, which is never safe for a woman who's been through childbirth and has a full bladder.

By the time we made it to our feet, our hands and knees were caked in mud, and I was worried about the dampness that surely had to be visible on the back of my dress. "Can you see anything?" I asked Lisa. When she began laughing so hard she couldn't breathe, I knew our movie-premiere night was over. We got back into the car and headed home.

Lisa—she is one of my safe-place sisters, the kind of friend with whom I can share embarrassment and accomplishment, joy and pain.

⤟

When I was released from the hospital in 1992, I left with a new realization that I desperately needed community. I needed a few friends I could trust, friends with whom I could share my darkest secrets. I also knew that I needed to begin lining my life up with the whole Word of God, not just the parts that made me comfortable. I spent so much of my time, either in seminary or in personal study, diving deep into God's Word, but I hadn't always understood how to apply this Living Word to my life.

Looking back on it, I can see my misstep, which I think other

The Word of

God is

alive

and able to speak

peace

to every one of our

concerns when we

stop, listen, and receive.

women fall into too: We can read the Bible and sign up for every Bible study our churches offer, but if there's no personal application, if we don't use the truths, we'll sink deeper into our struggles. We can memorize the text that encourages us to cast our cares on Christ, but if we don't stop and intentionally cast our cares on Him, the knowledge hasn't moved from the head to the heart. Whether you're worried about your children, your ability to pay your bills on time, the results of a medical test, or a million and one other struggles, the Word of God is alive and able to speak peace to every one of our concerns when we stop, listen, and receive. These truths are not only for ourselves but also for each other.

As I committed myself to studying Scripture about my personal need for a community of safe-place sisters, I discovered an overwhelming weight of wisdom.

> Therefore encourage one another and build one another up, just as you are doing. (1 Thess. 5:11 ESV)

> Two people are better off than one, for they can help each other succeed. If one person falls, the other can reach out and help. But someone who falls alone is in real trouble. Likewise, two people lying close together can keep each other warm. But how can one be warm alone? A person standing alone can be attacked and defeated, but two can stand back-to-back and conquer. Three are even better, for a triple-braided cord is not easily broken. (Eccl. 4:9–12)

> And let us consider how to stir up one another to love and good works, not neglecting to meet together, as is the habit of some, but encouraging one another, and all the more as you see the Day drawing near. (Heb. 10:24–25 ESV)

Let the word of Christ dwell in you richly, teaching and admonishing one another in all wisdom, singing psalms and hymns and spiritual songs, with thankfulness in your hearts to God. (Col. 3:16 ESV)

In his first letter to the Corinthians, Paul further unpacks the different gifts that each of us bring as the body of Christ, explaining why, though each part may be different, we need each other (1 Cor. 12). Scripture shows us that the healthiest way through this life is in community with one another.

I began to pray, asking God to lead me to the sisters I could commit to. I knew that as life moved on I'd have a larger circle of friends, as Christ had patterned with His twelve disciples but especially with Peter, James, and John. Like Jesus, I wanted to find a few I could invite into my secrets. I wanted safe-place sisters with whom I could break the silences that kept me so bound.

The first came as quite a surprise. In some ways we couldn't have been more different. We'd met years before when our differences were even more crystal clear. In fact, I discovered that was the whole point of our meeting. My record company couldn't decide how to introduce me to the American Christian public. Apparently, I didn't look very Christian. I had short black, spiky (sometimes purple) hair, I wore leather onstage, and I used fog and laser lights.

I remember being puzzled by their dilemma, asking why the content of my makeup case was more important than the content of my heart. The director of marketing said I'd understand if I could see myself in a room standing next to other Christian artists. I'd realize that I looked like a parrot at a hamster convention. I still didn't get it; this sounded like a compliment.

The record label came up with a solution. Each summer, a retreat was held at Estes Park in Colorado for the artists in the Christian music industry. Every evening the record companies would showcase their artists. Mine decided that the only way to expose everyone to the feathered wonder that was me was to ask the least likely artist if she would introduce me. So they asked Sandi Patty, and to her credit, Sandi said yes.

I liked her immediately. Her conservative dress made me look even more radical, but I couldn't have asked for a more grace-filled introduction that night. In the years following, we bumped into each other, and we'd catch up, but that was about the extent of our friendship until we ended up on a Christmas tour together. One night, when all the other girls had left the dressing room, Sandi asked if she could talk to me. She took a step of trust and poured out her heart, her brokenness, and the acute pain she'd hidden from so many—pain I'll guard to my dying day. We wept and prayed together. We hugged.

This woman I'd always seen as so perfect, so untouchable, carried an unbearable weight, and she asked if I might carry it with her. I reminded her that God's love for her had never been based on the fact that she was "Sandi Patty, one of the most successful Christian recording artists of the time." It was based on the truth that she is His daughter. She had sung that truth to thousands and thousands of people for years, but that night she needed someone to sing it back to her.

It's tempting to look at those around us and make assumptions about their lives. They look good. They seem to have everything under control. But sometimes the most perfect-looking people are the most in need of someone to see beyond what they present to the world. That is, of course, my story.

When Sandi opened up to me that night, I had no idea how much I would need her support in just a few short months. Three weeks after being released from the hospital, I appeared as an artist on a cruise to the Caribbean. I'd made the commitment the previous year and couldn't get out of my contract. I was raw and fragile, and the thought of being with five hundred happy cruising Christians was overwhelming. I stood in line to check onto the ship at the dock in Fort Lauderdale. Everyone was dressed in fun summer clothes and high-heeled sandals. I looked down and saw that I was wearing the moccasins I'd made in my craft class at the psych hospital.

Which one of these is not like the others?

Then she spotted me. Sandi was one of the other artists on board. She came over and pulled me out of the line. She told me that her manager had already taken care of my check-in, so we walked up the gangway onto the ship and straight to her cabin, where I unloaded.

"Okay," she said, "you don't want to be here right now, I get that, but here we are. So, my cabin is our safe place on this ship. When you want to run away, run here. When you want to cry, cry here."

We used that safe place many times on that trip. Some days I needed to be reminded that my worth wasn't built on the lies I had believed about myself, and some days she needed that same reminder. Her cabin became a holy place where confessing sisters knelt at the throne of grace and mercy together.

I met another sister, my don't-make-me-laugh-or-I'll-pee sister, at a Bible study she taught at our church in Nashville. Her class was, of course, the most popular one. She gave out chocolate and Starbucks cards and was an amazing teacher. I liked Lisa Harper instantly and enjoyed her company even though we were not close.

After Barry and I moved to Dallas, I didn't see much of her for a few years until we ended up sharing a platform as speakers and Bible teachers on the national Women of Faith tour. At times I found the packed arenas lonely places, places where I felt very lost among the large crowds. And during that tour, I found that there was more to my loneliness than the shame I'd carried from my past. I didn't know how to make friends. I didn't know how to ask for help. I was very good at being there for others, but my gut-level belief was that if I asked you to be my friend, you'd feel obliged to say yes even though you didn't want to. These were the lies I believed.

Part of my ongoing commitment to healing, however, was to reject the lies I'd believed for too long, so I decided to step out of what was comfortable. One night, during our team prayer time in the green-room before the conference began, I prayed this prayer out loud:

Father, I feel like I don't belong here. I'm surrounded by so many gifted women who love you, and every time I step up onto the stage I wonder if they agree with me that I don't belong. I don't want to live like this. I don't want my fear and insecurity to be greater than Your grace and mercy. Forgive me.

I had no idea that what felt like such a raw, unattractive prayer would open a floodgate of authentic pain from others. Almost every woman in that room shared that she felt the same way. We saw each other as having it all together, women without insecurity or self-doubt. That night, we became broken bread and poured-out wine in the hands of Christ to an audience who felt just as we did. We confessed our sin together, confessed our collective sense of insecurity, and somehow, we found healing.

Within that larger group of sisters, Lisa was the first one I told my biggest secret to. My friends knew that I'd been in a psych ward and that I still took medication, but Lisa was the one I told about my ongoing battle with suicidal thoughts. She heard my confession and hugged me as I cried through the darkness of it. She didn't hesitate to love me in that moment. She accepted me as I was and loved me where I was, always reminding me of the power of the Word of God.

This safe-sister relationship goes both ways, though. When she's needed it, I've helped carry her pain, too, such as when her journey to adopt a child turned into traumatic heartbreak. Twice, she was within days of receiving a child only to have the dream snatched away. She walked with one young mother through the full forty weeks of pregnancy before being informed that the child would go to another couple. I thought her heart would never mend from the grief and pain.

Then into that well of pain a woman spoke words that cut Lisa to the core, words that must have sounded so much like the words of Job's friends. It was "God's will" that the adoption failed, she said. The woman went further, explaining that because Lisa was a single woman with some brokenness in her childhood, she was probably too broken to raise a child alone. She suggested that Lisa go to the pound instead and get a dog. Those words cut. But worse than that, for a time, Lisa believed that lie. She even went to the pound and adopted Cookie, a large mixed-breed with soft eyes.

Lisa could have lived the rest of her life believing she was too broken to be a good mom, but those of us who loved her refused to let those lies take root. Over and over again we came against those lies. I prayed Scripture over her: "I will give her back her vineyards, and will make the Valley of Achor a door of hope" (Hos. 2:15 NIV). *Achor*, I knew, meant "despair" in the original language. And so, my constant prayer over Lisa was simple: *Lord Jesus, may this valley of Lisa's despair give way to a door of hope!*

I was with her the day she received the call that changed her life. We were in a meeting when her phone rang. She slipped out to take the call, so I knew it was important, but when she didn't come back after a longer time than usual, I went to find her. She was leaning against a wall with tears running down her face, still listening to whoever was on the other end. All I could do was put my arms around her and pray one word over and over again: "Jesus. Jesus. Jesus."

She could hardly speak when she finally got off the phone. A little girl in Haiti had just lost her mother to HIV/AIDS. There were no other relatives who could care for her, and if no one claimed this little girl, her health was so poor she wouldn't survive.

"They asked me to pray about it," she said through her tears. "I've been praying for thirty years, Sheila. I said yes."

Thirty minutes later, a photo of a scared, desperately thin little girl was texted to Lisa's phone. We both sobbed.

"That's my baby!" she said.

I flew into Nashville on the day she was finally able to bring Missy home from Haiti. For so long, I had walked with Lisa through her darkest hours, so I wanted to be one of the first faces she and Missy saw when they got off the plane. I wanted to be a reminder of the countless prayers we'd brought before God that now had been answered with this rich blessing. I wanted to welcome this darling child into our sisterhood, and share the joy of a homecoming. I also wanted to hug Lisa and celebrate her bravery—she'd listened to her sisters speak truth into the lies she'd believed and had chosen to believe only truth.

I looked at the arrivals board and saw that I had about thirty minutes until their plane landed. There was a toy store nearby, so I looked for something Missy might like. I settled on a pink purse in the shape of a poodle. I bought two little bracelets and put them inside the purse. My heart was racing in my chest as I saw the plane pull into the gate.

"Don't cry, don't cry!" I said to myself. "You'll scare the child."

The moment I saw Lisa's face and the darling little girl with colored beads in her hair in Lisa's arms, I couldn't contain myself. I hugged them tightly and breathed, "Welcome home, little one, welcome home." Lisa and I looked at each other. She had brought her daughter home.

When we believe lies about ourselves, it's easy to fall back into the pit of despair. We have an enemy who is not only a liar but also the accuser of God's children. He's not omniscient like our Father God. He doesn't know what we're thinking, but he's watched us fall often enough to know what our weakest places are. But this battle is not eternal. One day he will be thrown down forever. Scripture reminds us: "It has come at last—salvation and power and the Kingdom of our

God, and the authority of his Christ. For the accuser of our brothers and sisters has been thrown down to earth—the one who accuses them before our God day and night" (Rev. 12:10).

Until that day comes, we need to keep reminding each other of what's true. That's why our confession isn't relegated to our times with Jesus. That's why we invite people into our hidden places; that's why we tell our safe sisters about the secret shame and lies we're so prone to believe.

In community, we can confess to each other, pray for each other, and remind each other of the truths Christ has spoken to us in His living Word, the truths we've learned through our personal meditation. By reminding each other of these truths, we find healing in Christ through each other. We remind each other that we are loved just the way we are, and that shame and lies only thrive when we hide, when we withdraw to our hidden places. Shame and lies cannot survive the light of confession.

Shame and lies cannot
survive the light of confession.

But why is it important to confess our sins to each other? Surely God hears and forgives, doesn't He? In James, we read, "Confess your sins to each other and pray for each other so that you may be healed" (James 5:16).

The word that James uses here for *confess* means "to say out loud, to agree." Confessing to safe sisters takes away power from the enemy who loves to isolate us and keep us in the dark. There is also a fresh awareness of our sin when we confess to another. I can minimize my sin when I hold it to myself, but when I speak it out to another I face the serious weight of what my sin cost Christ.

I find the way Bonhoeffer reflects on mutual confession helpful: "A man [or a woman] who confesses his sins in the presence of a brother knows he is no longer alone with himself; he experiences the presence of God in the reality of the other person. As long as I am by myself in the confessions of my sins everything remains in the dark, but in the presence of a brother the sin has to be brought into the light."[1]

There is freedom in confessing out loud to a trusted sister who will love you and pray for you and hold you accountable to the life you want to live. But I urge you to be wise. Be careful whom you choose to share your story with and confess your sins to. Jesus said, "Don't throw your pearls to pigs! They will trample the pearls, then turn and attack you" (Matt. 7:6). In other words, don't take what's holy and sacred to you and give it those who may use it against you. That's why I urge you to ask the Holy Spirit to guide you to the right women. When you find those safe sisters, you've found the place to continue to be saved, to be the authentic you. It won't always be easy, but it will always be worth it.

Do you have a community of safe-place sisters? If you have those sisters who know and love you, who speak truth and hope to you when you're in the darkest of places, then hallelujah that you know this immense blessing. If you don't, I pray this will happen for you. More than that, I ask you to make this your daily prayer: "God, lead me into a community of safe sisters."

Then watch and listen to His voice. He will lead those sisters to you. And as He leads women to you, ask yourself whether the women will treat your life with care and compassion, whether they will ask and keep asking questions until you're ready to tell them the truth, whether they will love you no matter what. If they will, you've found your community of healing. Push into it.

Reflection

Something powerful happens when we confess our sins to each other. James 5:16 connects confession to healing, to making well again. That was certainly true for King David. When the prophet Nathan confronted him with his sin, it led not only to repentance but also to healing. This is how David described unconfessed sin: "When I refused to confess my sin, my body wasted away, and I groaned all day long" (Ps. 32:3). He then talks about the peace and joy that returns to a clean heart.

Do you bare your true self before God in prayer? Do you also share your innermost secrets with a safe sister? God promises to be present, and He will be faithful in response to your courage.

Chapter 9

❦

Get Back Up

Have you never heard?
Have you never understood?
The Lord is the everlasting God,
the Creator of all the earth.
He never grows weak or weary.
No one can measure the depths of his understanding.
He gives power to the weak
and strength to the powerless.
Even youths will become weak and tired,
and young men will fall in exhaustion.
But those who trust in the Lord will find new strength.
They will soar high on wings like eagles.
They will run and not grow weary.
They will walk and not faint.

—Isaiah 40:28–31

My sixtieth birthday came two weeks after Mum's funeral, and Barry and Christian did everything they could to make it special. Christian gave me a trophy that he'd hand-painted. My family tartan, or plaid, is the McNicol, and he had painted the base in those colors—green, blue, red, and yellow. On the front he'd added, "World's Best Mom." Barry gave me a gorgeous pink-leather jacket that I'd been eyeing for months.

If we had stopped with these two gifts, it would have been enough. But Barry had another waiting for me. I opened it, and it was obvious he'd been working on it for some time. It was a large brown-leather album with the message "You Are Loved" embossed in gold on the cover.

The first page held a card on which he'd written, "If I know what love is, it's because of you." The second page contained a letter from Christian. I'll keep most of it tucked away in my heart except this one line: "You understand what Christianity is supposed to be: a hospital for the broken, not a museum for the perfect." What a beautiful thought. I turned the page, and then the next, and then the next. Page after page contained beautiful letters from friends around the world. It was such a priceless gift.

It was a lovely day, and I did everything I could to fight the sadness. But it was my first birthday without Mum, and I missed the sound of her voice on the other end of the line. Every year when Mum called on my birthday, I'd ask her to sing "Happy Birthday" to me. She didn't have a very good singing voice, but I loved her rendition of the old birthday standard, and my heart hurt that I wouldn't hear it that day.

Somehow, not having my mum anymore made me feel older. A week before her death my brother's card arrived from England. It said, "Sheila, don't worry—you're only sixty!" My stomach turned, and my response was visceral. "No I am not!" I said aloud to no one in particular.

I put the card facedown on the kitchen counter and went upstairs. Two minutes later I came back down, picked up the card, and put it in my desk drawer.

Again, I found myself talking to the air. "I am not sixty! Mum's sixty." As the initial shock wore off, I worked out that Mum was, in fact, about to turn eighty-eight.

When I think of Mum at sixty, I remember her as older than I think of myself now. Perhaps that's partly because she's always gone with the traditional Scottish shampoo-and-set hairdo. In my teenage years, every Friday night I'd wash Mum's hair over the kitchen sink, then roll it up in wee rollers like mini hot dogs. I'd sit her in a chair and attach an inflatable hood to a hair dryer. Then I'd comb out her hair and spray it down with something that felt like vaporized glue. After that treatment, she was good for a week.

As far as her attire went, Mum didn't wear skinny jeans at sixty. Mind you, Mum didn't wear any kind of jeans. My mum and my nana (her mum) held age-appropriate modesty almost as close as the Word of God. If my nana saw a woman trying to look younger than she was, she called it "mutton dressed as lamb." I looked at my brother's card again and made a mental note to reevaluate my wardrobe.

My brother's card arrived weeks before my birthday, but it also reminded me that I needed to mail Mum's birthday gifts so they'd get to Scotland on time. I'd bought a sweater with red cardinals embroidered on the front. A friend once told me that red cardinals appear when they sense the presence of angels, and so, it somehow seemed fitting that this was my mother's favorite bird. I felt as though she'd become a sweet angel in her older age.

I'd also framed a recent photo of Christian, so that when she remembered him, she wouldn't think of him as a little boy. I wanted her to have a tangible reminder of what an amazing man he has grown to be. I wrapped the gifts in silver and pink paper, wrote her a card, and put them on the chair by the door to mail the following day. That was the morning my sister called to tell me that Mum had died.

As the days wore on, I recognized the warning signals that indicated I wasn't doing well. It wasn't just about Mum's death. I was slipping, sliding down into the dark well. It's hard to explain clinical depression if you've never struggled with it. It's more than just a few bad days in a row. I've walked with friends through depression that is situational. If you lose a job or a relationship, you can often find yourself plunged into a dark space. If you're struggling financially or with your health, those are challenges that can cast dark shadows over your soul, but usually, in time, they will pass.

Clinical depression is a different sort of animal. It's a constant mind trip, a perpetual loop of dark thought spurred by the absence of certain necessary hormones—in my case, serotonin, to be exact.

Over the years, I'd learned about tools that could help me stay on an even keel when my serotonin levels spun into the death spiral. Medication, prayer, exercise, the Word of God—all these have helped me in my day-to-day life. But after Mum's death, none of these tools seemed to help anymore. I found it hard to concentrate. I couldn't sleep. I began to pull away from people. And though I knew that I needed my community of sisters to help me walk into the light, all I wanted to do was crawl back into my hiding place to be alone. I wanted to close my eyes and shut the door.

I was thirty-six when I had my first breakdown. Now I was sixty, and it felt as if I was spinning back into a similar crisis. I needed to know if everything I believed about my relationship with God was true. I needed to know if confessing my darkest feelings to Christ, letting go of the shame, meditating on His great love for me, and confessing to my safe-place sisters—all of it—was really the solution for my healing. Or were these practices only crutches to help me limp by?

I knew what the next step was. It was ironic. Months before, I had put a plan in place. But to be honest, the plan wasn't intended for me. Instead, it was an offering for anyone who wrote me asking for help. And when I'd written it, I didn't know that I would be the one needing help.

I pulled up the document on my computer—"You Are Loved"—and read the scripture at the top of the page.

And so, dear brothers and sisters, I plead with you to give your bodies to God because of all he has done for you. Let them be a living and holy sacrifice—the kind he will find acceptable. This is truly the way to worship him. Don't copy the behavior and customs of this world, but let God transform you into a new person by changing the way you think. Then you will learn to know God's will for you, which is good and pleasing and perfect. (Rom. 12:1–2)

I read the verse and noticed the catchy little illustration I'd jotted beneath it. In the Old Testament, the priests did not consult the animals who were about to be sacrificed to see if they felt it was a good day to die. Instead, the call was made, the animal was slaughtered, and that was that. Yet we're called to be living sacrifices, to give up our own choices, fears, and despair and follow God to the altar, remaining there without question no matter how hot or uncomfortable it gets.

I considered how annoying that illustration might be to someone in real pain, someone suffering under the weight of clinical depression, someone like me. But even still, I couldn't get away from the power of the scripture. I wanted to know: What does it mean to be a living and holy sacrifice? The deeper I dug into the text, the more it became clear that my illustration was way off.

The English Standard Version of the Bible translates Romans 12:1 this way: "I appeal to you therefore, brothers, by the mercies of God, to *present* your bodies as a living sacrifice, holy and acceptable to God, which is your spiritual worship" (emphasis mine).

The verb *present* here in the Greek means "to present once and for all." It's a weighty, once-in-a-lifetime event. The way a wife would commit to a husband, or more profoundly, the way Christ committed to the road to the cross. It means setting your face in one direction and never looking back, even amid pain, suffering, or clinical depression. It means that even when we fall in the middle of life's mess, we get back up, and we keep walking in sacrificial worship and obedience to Christ.

When we fall in the middle of life's mess,
we get back up, and we keep walking in
sacrificial worship and obedience to Christ.

I needed to know more. What does it mean to be holy, set apart? I kept digging. In the Old Testament sacrificial system, gold and silver were used to make vessels that were used in the temple alone. There were many other gold and silver pieces, but those specific pieces were set apart for God. That's who we are. When we surrender our lives to Christ, we're pulled out of the world. We don't belong to ourselves anymore, and we don't belong to our secrets or shame. Instead we're set apart to bring God glory. And in this surrender, we live every day—even the darkest of days—as an act of worship to Him.

I thought of Christ in the Garden of Gethsemane throwing Himself on the mercy of His Father. "If it is possible . . . Yet I want your will to be done, not mine," He said (Matt. 26:39). Wrung from the depths of Christ's soul came this simple truth: Although all things are possible with God, not all things are His will. Jesus knew this, and He presented Himself to God as the ultimate sacrifice. He pushed through the darkness and into God's will. I sat with that for a while.

Could God take my depression away? Absolutely. But even if He didn't, I was called to present myself as a sacrifice even still. I am called to worship Him through it. I am called to follow the way of Jesus, to sacrifice my own attempts to secret away the pain, and to practice confession, meditation, and community.

I suppose the same applies to you. Could God have made your husband stay? Yes. Will you worship Him through that dark night if he doesn't come home?

Could God have saved your family from bankruptcy? Yes. Will you still worship Him as you let go of all the things you thought you needed?

Could God have given you a child? Yes. Will you worship Him if that door is closed?

Could God have made you taller, thinner, smarter? Yes. But will you still worship Him now as the real, authentic you?

When we do, we find strength for this beautiful, broken life. It will never be perfect, but it can be beautiful.

As I considered Romans 12:1, I thought of so many of you who've shared parts of your story with me. At times you've asked, "Where are You, God?" I was asking that same question that day as I closed my computer and knelt on the dining-room carpet. I remembered my favorite waiting verse and rolled it over in my head: "They who wait for the LORD shall renew their strength" (Isa. 40:31 ESV). And with new resolve, I told Him, *I am here. I am here.* And in that waiting, I heard nothing, not at first. Instead, the story of the great preacher, Charles Spurgeon, came to mind.

Spurgeon was known as the prince of preachers. In his twenties, he pastored the largest Protestant mega-church, but he struggled for most of his life with acute bouts of depression. I'm so grateful that he wrote and spoke about it. If mental illness has limited curb appeal in our day and age, can you imagine how hard it was to talk about in the mid-nineteenth century? The following is an excerpt from one of my favorite sermons of his, titled "Songs in the Night."

It is easy to sing when we can read the notes by daylight; but he is the skillful singer who can sing when there is not a ray of light by which to read, who sings from his heart, and not from a book that he can see, because he has no means of reading, save from that inward book of his own living spirit, whence notes of gratitude pour forth in songs of praise.[1]

His love for those who flocked to hear him preach is clear. For me his grace-filled words encouraged me to pour out every single drop of grief or fear or anger to God. He reminded me again that God is my safe place.

> O dear friend, when thy grief presses thee to the very dust, worship there! If that spot has come to be thy Gethsemane, then present there thy "strong crying and tears" unto thy God. Remember David's words, "Ye people, pour out your hearts,"—but do not stop there, finish the quotation,—"Ye people, pour out your hearts before him." Turn the vessel upside down; it is a good thing to empty it, for this grief may ferment into something more sour. Turn the vessel upside down, and let every drop run out; but let it be before the Lord.[2]

Such profound wisdom. Turn the vessel upside down; let every drop of grief or fear pour out. Let it pour out before the Lord. And there, in the darkest hour, as I waited for relief, that's what I did.

I poured it out to God, yes; I invited Him into my secret room. And as I meditated on His great love for me, there was great relief. Even still, I knew that I had to confess my darkness to a friend, to say out loud, "I need help." I needed someone to speak the truth to me, to combat the lies that plagued me—*It'd be better if I'd never been born, or if God took me home, or if I ended it all*—and remind me that I was a well-loved child of God. I'd learned the grace available when I was able to say, "I need You."

So, though I didn't feel like crawling out of bed, like getting showered and dressed and being around people, I did what it took to clean myself up. I dragged myself to a local church where another safe-place sister, Lisa Bevere, was speaking.

I entered the church and grabbed a moment to hug Lisa before the evening began. She turned to face me and asked how I was doing. I told her, "Not great."

"At the end, don't leave. I'm serious, Sheila, don't leave," she said.

She shared a beautiful message that night on connection, why we need each other, and how Christ modeled that for us. At the end, after she'd greeted people, she put her arm through mine and led me into the private room she'd been given. She looked into my eyes and through tears said, "I know, I know!"

I knelt on the floor and poured my heart out to her as she held me. She laid hands on me and prayed, and it brought such healing. She confronted the lies of my depression, reminded me that she loves me no matter how dark I feel. She finally reminded me of the ultimate truth—that even in my darkness, I am a dearly loved little girl.

There is a mystery in the gift of the body of Christ. We're on holy ground when we confess our sins to one another and pray for each other, when we remind each other of the truth. And this begs the question, at least for me: Is depression sin? Not at all, but it is wrong to believe the lies depression implants in my soul. Depression tells me that I have no future or hope, and that life will swallow me up. But in Christ, I know those are lies. He is my future and hope. He is the enemy of fear and despair. He brings me life. As the psalmist says,

> The LORD is my light and my salvation;
>   whom shall I fear?
> The LORD is the stronghold of my life;
>   of whom shall I be afraid? (Ps. 27:1 ESV)

Though I have always loved that verse, I could never pray the last two verses of Psalm 27. But I have learned that when I share my secrets and shame within my safe community, I hear the community of safe sisters claiming those verses for me: "I believe that I shall look upon the goodness of the LORD in the land of the living! Wait for the LORD; be strong, and let your heart take courage; wait for the LORD!" (27:13–14 ESV). When I hear the voices of my sweet sisters, when I feel their love, I know the truth. I really will see the goodness of the Lord in the land of the living; I really can be strong and take courage as I wait for Him.

Christ has shown us a path to lead us home. Whether it's light or dark, it is faithful—we recognize our position, confess it to God, meditate on His love, and despise any shame that might keep us in bondage. Then we may bring our confession to our safe-place sisters and walk into the truth. This act of despising shame is the path of Christ:

> Therefore, since we are surrounded by so great a cloud of witnesses, let us also lay aside every weight, and sin which clings so closely, and let us run with endurance the race that is set before us, looking to Jesus, the founder and perfecter of our faith, who for the joy that was set before him endured the cross, despising the shame, and is seated at the right hand of the throne of God. (Heb. 12:1–2 ESV)

The Greek word used for *despising* is the word *kataphroneó*, which means "to think little of or to pay little attention to." How could Christ bear the shame of carrying all the sin of the world, of being stripped naked and executed in the worst possible way? The answer is simple: He knew the truth about who He was. He knew His identity. He was the well-loved Son of God, called for a purpose.

No matter what's been taken from you, no one can take away your identity in Christ. You are a well-loved daughter of the King, and you've been called for a purpose. You can meditate on this truth, know it down to your bones. You can despise the shame of the secrets and lies you've believed. You can confess them to your safe-place sisters and listen as they remind you that your shame has been released through the power of Christ's cross. You can follow in the footsteps of Jesus.

❧

The morning following my conversation with Lisa, I sat outside with a cup of coffee in our little garden. Our dogs were chasing a squirrel

No matter

what's been

Taken

from you,

no one can

take away your

identity

in Christ.

until they tired themselves out and settled at my feet. I felt safe—not fixed but safe. I felt loved—not fixed but loved. Leaves were beginning to fall from the trees. It was a peaceful morning.

Our Yorkie, Maggie, suddenly sat up, staring at a hole through the large oak tree at the bottom of our yard. I thought at first the squirrel was back until I saw the flash of brilliant color. It was a red cardinal, and the thoughts of my mother came racing back. But this time, there was not a hint of darkness—only light. I raised my cup of coffee heavenward and said, "Thank You."

Reflection

It's easy to be conformed to the world without thinking about it. Fashions come and go, trends come and go, but we're called to reject those outward pressures. German theologian Franz Leenhardt put it this way: "What madness it is to join in this puppet show which is displayed on a tottering stage."[3]

In Romans 12:1–2, Paul encourages us to let God transform us into new people by changing the way we think. The call is to start thinking God's thoughts and to see ourselves as He sees us. Changing our perspective takes work.

The change is a radical reorientation that begins deep within the human heart, and it takes place moment by moment as we say yes to God.

When we feel unloved we can declare: *I am a well-loved daughter of the King of kings.*

When we're discouraged, believing we'll never make any lasting change, we remind ourselves: *Christ has committed to finishing the work He began in us.*

When we feel alone, we remind ourselves: *"For God has said, 'I will never fail you. I will never abandon you'"* (Heb. 13:5).

Are there areas that you can identify where obedience to

Christ and the Word is a struggle? Write them down and ask the Holy Spirit to help you understand why these areas are hard for you. If you choose to draw a little cross on your wrist, it might serve as a reminder that we—the children of the cross—don't live for this world.

Chapter 10

> *Bran thought about it. "Can a man still be brave if he's afraid?"*
> *"That is the only time a man can be brave," his father told him.*
>
> —GEORGE R.R. MARTIN, *A GAME OF THRONES*

You Are Braver Than You Know

I remember exactly where I was sitting when Luci called. I was at a table in the mall outside my favorite coffee shop working on a new book.

"Sheila, it's Luci. Do you have a minute?" she asked.

"Sure, Luc, what do you need?"

"Are you free next Wednesday? If you are, I wondered if you'd have any interest in coming with me to have coffee with Bono?" she asked.

"Excuse me. Can you hold just a moment?"

I put the phone down on the table, ran into the nearest store, and let out a primal yell. I hustled back to my table, collected myself, picked up the phone, and said, "That would be lovely."

I have been a fan of U2 from their earliest years. We even shared a stage once. In 1981, I was headlining with my band at Greenbelt, a music and arts festival in England. That evening, before I took the stage, the promoters introduced a new band from Ireland, and the rest is history.

The following Wednesday, I picked up Luci and our friend Mary Graham, and we drove downtown to the funky boutique hotel where Bono was staying. Luci told me that the invitation had come because she was a supporter of the ONE Campaign, a global initiative cofounded by Bono that worked to eradicate poverty.

"I seemed to remember you like U2?" Luci said as we walked into the lobby.

"Like them! Luci, that's like saying God's quite a nice person. The sentiment doesn't really come close!"

I'd hoped we'd meet him in the restaurant so that I could dash in and sit down before I fell over, but he was waiting for us in the lobby.

"Hello, I'm Bono," he said, stretching out his hand.

Dear Jesus, help me now.

"Hi, I'm Sheila, and this as you probably know is Luci Swindoll and Mary Graham," I said, about two octaves too high.

"We have a room upstairs, but the elevator's a bit small," he said. "We'll have to go two at a time. Luci, do you want to ride up with me?" he asked.

"Why don't you go up with Sheila?" she said.

That is the day Luci worked herself into my will.

In the room, Bono talked about his passion for justice, and he quoted from the book of Isaiah. He asked us about our work with World Vision and our recent trips to Africa and India. It's a memory I will always treasure.

A couple of weeks later, he sent us a gift. It was a video message to the fifteen thousand women gathered with us at a Women of Faith event in an arena that night. He talked about the power of women to change the world, and then he addressed Luci, Mary, and me by name. He called us "lionesses for Jesus."

The following day I went to a toy store and bought a little toy lioness. I brought her home and studied her face, the strength in her paws, muscles ready to pounce if anyone threatened her young, then I carefully placed her in my desk drawer. I couldn't identify with such a fierce beauty. My understanding of strength needed work.

Time passed, and a year before Mum's death I was back in that same arena. Before the evening's event began, Judy, our tour intercessor, asked if she could speak privately with me for a few moments. She said that when she was praying for me, God told her to tell me that it was time for battle. She told me not to be afraid because I had everything I needed. She anointed me with oil, laid hands on me, and prayed for me.

"This is how God sees you," she said.

She gave me a picture. It was of a roaring lion heading into battle carrying a young girl on his back. The girl's sword is drawn, ready to attack, but she is blindfolded, the tail of that blindfold flapping in the wind. The bronze shield on her left arm displayed the scales of justice, perfectly balanced.

"I don't understand, Judy," I said. "Why is she blindfolded?"

"Because she's not going in her own strength. Her strength and power are in the Lion of Judah."

As I studied that picture, something began to stir in me. I thought back to my favorite childhood books, The Chronicles of Narnia by C. S. Lewis. I imagine you might have seen the movies that were made in the early 2000s, but I'm rather fond of the televised series produced in 1988 by the BBC in England. The series wasn't as glossy as the movies, but its depiction of British childhood was familiar to me—such as the sensible shoes the children wore and the games they played.

The character I've always identified with is Lucy. Her sister, Susan, was the traditional beauty of the family with long flowing hair, but Lucy and I shared a bowl haircut. My love for Lucy was deeper than a shared hairdo, though. Lucy had a gentle way and was kind to all the animals in Narnia. They trusted her. In many ways she was the least likely warrior, and yet because of her simple faith

Our true

identity

is found in the

love of God,

not in the *labels*

that we've worn.

she could see Aslan—the wild and fearsome lion ruler—when the others couldn't.

As a child, I wanted to be Lucy. I wanted to know Aslan.

I thanked Judy for the picture, not knowing what had prompted her to give it to me. Even still, I was thankful for the reminder.

A few months after Mum's death I was looking through my desk drawer for my passport. I'd put it there after I returned from Scotland, but I couldn't find it. I pulled the drawer out and turned it upside down, and there she was—my little lioness. I set her beside the picture Judy had given me and smiled. It was as if God was asking me, "Do you understand?"

I sat quietly in God's presence, considering His voice, the lioness, the picture. The pieces began to fall into place. I thought back to who I was as a young child, how I climbed trees and rescued stray dogs. Mum told me I was fearless. I was Lucy, brave and kind, the kid who could see God. That's how God made me, even if I forgot for a while. But as I sat in the quiet, God's presence reminded me. And as He reminded me, I felt brave, strong, and dearly loved by my Father God.

Becoming fully who we were made to be means remembering who we really are and believing the truth instead of the lies life has led us to believe. Our true identity is found in the love of God, not in the labels that we've worn.

I'm not "Sheila Walsh, whose father committed suicide."

I'm not "Sheila Walsh, the psych patient."

I'm not "Sheila Walsh, the shameful."

I'm Sheila Walsh, a well-loved daughter of the King of kings.

Have I always felt that? No. Did that mean it wasn't always true? No.

I wonder how you identify yourself. Do you define yourself by your circumstances? Do you define yourself as divorced, or fat, or financially troubled? Do you define yourself by your singleness, your loneliness? Do you see yourself as forgotten or passed over? Do you define yourself by the mess you're in the middle of, right now? It's easy to believe the labels we've been handed or the lies about our identities, but God doesn't define us by our assumed collection of labels. He doesn't define us by our weakness. When God looks at us, He sees well-loved daughters.

Meditate on that truth, even now.

The apostle Paul knew that God didn't define him by his weakness. In his second letter to the Corinthians, he wrote of a "thorn in the flesh," which he begged God to take away. What was his thorn? Some say he was losing his eyesight, or that he had malaria. Some claim he was tormented by severe migraines. Others think it was ongoing persecution from the Jewish religious community or the shame he carried from his early persecution of the church. Whatever it was—and no one knows for certain—it caused Paul acute pain. Paul wrote, "Three times I pleaded with the Lord about this, that it should leave me. But he said to me, 'My grace is sufficient for you, for my power is made perfect in weakness'" (2 Cor. 12:8–9 ESV).

Why wouldn't God take these things away? I don't know. Perhaps the thorn was a mercy in disguise, which reminded Paul of just how much he needed Christ. Perhaps the thorn humanized him, made it easier for him to relate to others who were struggling. Isn't it hard to be comforted by someone who has never suffered? Whatever the case may be, Paul knew his identity—he was a powerful son of God, despite his weakness.

What do you see as your thorn, the secret shame that's stopping you from living into your God-given identity as a dearly loved little girl? What if, like Paul, we asked God to show Himself powerful in these weaknesses? The truth is, where our surrendered brokenness meets God's mercy, power flows like a mighty river.

The truth is, where our surrendered brokenness meets God's mercy, power flows like a mighty river.

But this begs the question: Apart from the community of safe sisters, how do we remember our true identity when we feel so weak? How do we guard ourselves from the thorny lies the enemy of our souls might use to disrupt our lives, to make us forget our true identity?

The answer is simple: We take up our weapons. The tricky part, though, is that our weapons don't look like weapons, just as our strength doesn't look like strength.

Consider Christ's ultimate weapon—His death on the cross. To the onlookers at Golgotha that day, the cross looked like a defeat. They had no way of knowing that it was the mightiest weapon ever wielded, and it was in the hand of God. In his fantastic commentary on the gospel of John, J. C. Ryle wrote, "The form of the cross is that of a sword with the point downward; above is the hilt toward heaven, as if in the hand of God; below is the point toward earth, as if thrust through the head of the old serpent the devil."[1]

In the same way, our weapons don't look threatening to human eyes, but in the spiritual realm, they are recognized as mighty. We use confession, prayer, meditation, and community alongside silence, obedience, and gratitude. Scripture teaches us that we also use forgiveness, grace, love, and mercy. And perhaps that brings us to this point—the greatest of all, the Word of God itself.

Paul gives a description of God's armor:

> Stand firm then, with the belt of truth buckled around your waist, with the breastplate of righteousness in place, and with your feet fitted with the readiness that comes from the gospel of peace. In addition to all this, take up the shield of faith, with which you can extinguish all the flaming arrows of the evil one. Take the helmet of salvation and the sword of the Spirit, which is the word of God. (Eph. 6:14–17 NIV)

Many excellent books have been written on the whole armor of God, so I won't attempt to unpack it piece by piece. That said, there is something so powerful about "the sword of the Spirit, which is the word of God" that I'd never understood before. The more I unpacked it, the richer my understanding.

In the Ephesians passage, the word Paul uses for *sword* is the Greek word *machairan*. It's a feminine word, used for a short sword or dagger. It's not the kind of sword you would wield going into a general battle. Instead, the word implies a much more personal weapon, one used in hand-to-hand combat.

The word used for *word* of God is the Greek word *rhema*. That's not the word used when Scripture is referring to Christ—the Word—or the Bible as a whole. This is a word used for a short phrase, a statement, an expression, or a saying. In other words, Paul is letting us know that the way we do battle is to have our daggers ready. We combat the enemy of God with specific promises or verses from the Word of God. Christ modeled what that looks like.

The only place in Scripture where we're given a picture of God in three persons present at the same time is at Christ's baptism: "When Jesus was baptized, immediately he went up from the water, and behold, the heavens were opened to him, and he saw the Spirit of God descending like a dove and coming to rest on him; and behold, a voice from heaven said, 'This is my beloved Son, with whom I am well pleased'" (Matt. 3:16–17 ESV).

God declared Christ's identity as a dearly loved Son over Him, and then the Spirit led Jesus into the wilderness to be tempted by the devil for forty days. This wilderness—it was a lonely barren place on the rocky slopes of the Judean mountains toward the Dead Sea. It was a place where robbers and revolutionaries met. Most people avoided the wilderness. But Jesus followed the Spirit in faith.

For forty days, Christ wandered the desert without food or friends. And Scripture teaches us that at the end of those forty days, when Jesus was tired and hungry, the devil came to Jesus to tempt Him. First, the enemy questioned Christ's identity and tempted His physical need: "If you are the Son of God," Satan said, "tell this stone to become a loaf of bread" (Luke 4:3).

Christ knew who He was—God's dearly loved Son—and He picked up a dagger from Deuteronomy 8, saying, "People do not live by bread alone" (Luke 4:4).

Satan next turned to what was, perhaps, the cruelest temptation of all—the temptation to gain the kingdom without the suffering. Scripture puts it this way: "And the devil took him up and showed him all the kingdoms of the world in a moment of time, and said to him, 'To you I will give all this authority and their glory, for it has been delivered to me, and I give it to whom I will. If you, then, will worship me, it will all be yours'" (Luke 4:5–7 ESV).

Satan offered Jesus an easy way out. But Christ, even in a weakened state, refused. He responded with a verse from Deuteronomy 6: "You shall worship the Lord your God, and him only shall you serve" (Luke 4:8 ESV).

Finally, the enemy took Jesus to Jerusalem and brought Him to the pinnacle of the temple, which overlooked the city and surrounding countryside. He said, "If you are the Son of God, throw yourself down from here, for it is written, 'He will command his angels concerning you, to guard you,' and 'On their hands they will bear you up, lest you strike your foot against a stone'" (Luke 4:9–11 ESV).

Here the enemy quoted Psalm 91, but he quoted verses that suited his purposes. He missed verse 9, which says, "Because you have made the LORD your dwelling place" (ESV).

The enemy of God can tempt us with parts of the Word of God. That's why it's so important that we know the Word so that we can pick up our weapons. Christ knew the Word well, and He wielded his third weapon, quoting Deuteronomy 6:16: "You shall not put the Lord your God to the test" (Luke 4:12 ESV).

The Son of God used the Word of God to combat the enemy of

God. This is how we fight. We might look as if we are standing alone, but the Lion of Judah, the great Aslan, is with us. He gives us the weapons we need to combat the lies our enemy might speak over us or our safe sisters. This, I suppose, brings us to this question: What are the weapons you need for your fight? What are the weapons your sisters need for their own battles, their own personal messes? How does the enemy test us?

Consider these promises, these carefully chosen daggers from the Word of God to fight against the lies that come against you and your safe-place sisters.

> *If you struggle with depression:* "Yet I am confident I will see the LORD's goodness while I am here in the land of the living" (Ps. 27:13).

> *If you struggle with fear:* "Fear not, for I am with you; be not dismayed, for I am your God; I will strengthen you, I will help you, I will uphold you with my righteous right hand" (Isa. 41:10 ESV).

> *If God seems distant:* "For I am sure that neither death nor life, nor angels nor rulers, nor things present nor things to come, nor powers, nor height nor depth, nor anything else in all creation, will be able to separate us from the love of God in Christ Jesus our Lord" (Rom. 8:38–39 ESV).

> *If you're afraid about what's happening in the world:* "God is our refuge and strength, a very present help in trouble" (Ps. 46:1 ESV).

There are more than three thousand promises in God's Word. I encourage you to take the time to hone your weapons. Don't wait until the next storm hits to prepare: Get ready now. Copy them out on cards or commit them to memory. Then when you or one of your safe-place sisters is under attack, you'll have the daggers by your side.

There is power in the Word of God. I need that power and strength, especially when I don't have my friends with me to encourage me. Some nights when I step up onto a platform to speak I don't feel at my best, but I rest in the truth that the Word of God never has a bad day. I've literally been walking onto a stage or pulpit and heard the enemy whisper, "You're too tired, you can't do this, and you've got nothing to offer." I stop. I pause right there with people watching, wondering what's wrong with me, and I pull out my weapon: "I can do everything through Christ, who gives me strength" (Phil. 4:13).

Then I walk on, not strong in myself but not alone because I'm with Christ.

What does it look like to wield your personalized dagger? There's a powerful visual of what that looks like in the film adaptation of the fourth book in The Chronicles of Narnia, *Prince Caspian*. It's not 100 percent true to the book, but it's quite lovely anyway. In the film, Lucy says to Aslan, "I wish I was braver."

Aslan replies, "If you were any braver, you would be a lioness."

So Lucy walks alone onto the bridge and faces the vast Telmarine army. The army stops for a moment, stunned to see a young girl blocking their way. It's a David and Goliath moment. With a small smile, Lucy draws out her dagger and waves it at them. That's when Aslan begins to pace with deliberate steps just behind her, and we know why she's not afraid. She's not alone. Neither are we.

I believe what Bono told the crowd that day: "A woman who understands her worth in Christ can change the world." To put it another way, as Mr. Beaver remarked in *The Lion, the Witch and the Wardrobe*, "Aslan is on the move."

Let it be true in, through, and around us.

Reflection

Our lives sometimes take sudden left turns, and we find ourselves in a new town, a new job, or a new church, and we don't know anyone. Some of us become isolated by illness or divorce, and the structure that was once in place has been ripped away from under us. There will be times, too, when our safe sisters are not there for us. What do we do then? What do we do when we not only feel alone but are alone and life is a mess?

On days like that, it's difficult to even pray. So I go to this scripture: "The Holy Spirit helps us in our weakness. For example, we don't know what God wants us to pray for. But the Holy Spirit prays for us with groanings that cannot be expressed in words. And the Father who knows all hearts knows what the Spirit is saying, for the Spirit pleads for us believers in harmony with God's own will" (Rom. 8:26–27).

I love that. He pleads for us. He's got our back. We'll make it through this messy, beautiful, broken life.

I've also built up my arsenal with a few truths that I want to share with you, too, so that you may use them in your battles. I've written them on cards that I keep on the inside of my wallet.

I'm not home yet.
Tears are okay.
Tomorrow the sun will rise again.
God is with me whether I feel His presence or not.
Silence can be offered as worship.
I am loved.

I read these over and over—as often as needed—then tuck them back inside my wallet. Do these words ring true for you? Which statement speaks to you the most? What others can you add to your arsenal?

Chapter 11

꧁꧂

Fully Known and Fully Loved

"But forget all that—
it is nothing compared to what I am going to do.
For I am about to do something new.
See, I have already begun! Do you not see it?
I will make a pathway through the wilderness.
I will create rivers in the dry wasteland."

—Isaiah 43:18–19

I never knew my father in his good days. At this point in my life, I've come to grips with that. I have a few photographs but no real memories of the happy father he was before his aneurysm. This being the case, on the day of Mum's funeral I was given a rare gift.

We'd invited all who attended her service to join us for a reception in a nearby hotel. I moved around the room trying to make sure I said hello to everyone. I saw a gentleman who I didn't recognize getting ready to leave, so I went over and introduced myself.

"Thank you so much for coming," I said. "I'm Sheila, Betty's daughter."

"I know who you are, lass," he said. "You did a beautiful job

137

in the church today. Paying tribute to your mother couldn't have been easy."

"Thank you, sir. Were you a friend of Mum's?" I asked.

"I was a friend of your dad's, lass," he said.

I took a step back for a moment. I was shocked. I'd never met any of Dad's friends. After his death we left town and moved from Cumnock to Ayr, just fifteen miles away, back to where the rest of Mum's family lived. It was a short geographical distance, but it was home to her. Mum had decided there were too many terrible memories for her in Cumnock. What's more, Dad had no family left to tell me anything about what he was like as a boy. There were no photos of him growing up, nothing to give me any inkling about his personality. But there in that hotel was someone who knew my dad, someone who was getting ready to leave. I asked if he'd stay for just a few more minutes, but he told me he had to go.

He paused for a minute, then took my hands in his and said, "You've grown into a beautiful woman. I knew your dad very well. He would have been so proud of you!"

With that, he was gone. I know he meant those words as a gift, but they felt like a knife in my heart.

If he'd survived, he really would have loved you!

I left the dining room and found a little privacy in the ladies' room. The stranger's words rang over and over in my head. I'd longed to hear those words all my life, but I wanted to hear them from my dad, not from his friend.

There was no one else in the restroom, so I confessed how I felt to God.

"That made me so sad," I said. "Dad would have been proud of me? How would that have changed my life?" I talked on and on, spoke aloud what I felt.

As I've learned that God is my safe place, I've learned to confess all my secret pain, all my unspoken hurts. It doesn't mean there won't be pain; it just means I won't keep it hidden any longer. I'll bring it all into His presence—the sorrow, questions, anger, sadness. I bring the joy and laughter too. Every emotion, every feeling, every thought is welcomed. And so, in that bathroom, I turned to my safe place.

I sat quietly for a while. I asked God to speak to the darkness. In the stillness I heard my Father speak to the deepest, safest place inside me.

I'm proud of you. I love you so much. I've never missed a moment of your life. I've been there all along, and I'm right here now.

I hadn't known it, but this was what I'd been waiting for. This was what I wanted to hear and know. I raised my arms as if in worship, but it felt more like a daughter raising her arms to her dad so that he could pick her up. I felt like letting go—of the anger, sorrow, and pain. It felt like what I can only describe as joy—pure, undiluted joy.

There, in that bathroom, I thought back on so many of the moments when I'd felt alone. I remembered summer camp one year, when the dads were invited to spend the day with their kids. I hid in my room until it was over. I remembered walking along the beach when I was sixteen years old. Mum was in surgery and I knew it was serious, and I was afraid of being left alone. So many moments played before my eyes like an old black-and-white movie reel. I realized that I've always seen myself as a lonely girl. But there, I was learning the truth: though I felt lonely and scared, I was the well-loved girl of God.

And though these feelings of loneliness were familiar, I was coming into an understanding: just because a place has become familiar doesn't mean it's where you belong.

I dried my eyes and went back into the dining room. Christian had been looking for me.

"Are you okay, Mom?"

"I am," I said. "I'm really good."

It would have been nice if that post-funeral bathroom moment had fixed me, if it had warded off the dark days that were to come in the months following the funeral. But it takes time for truth to

Just because a

place

has become

familiar

doesn't mean

it's where you

belong.

replace embedded lies. It's easy to sink back into old ways of thinking, old pictures of how you see yourself. And looking back on it, I suppose this is what happened to me after I returned to the States. It took me months to figure out that confession, silence, meditation, and a community of safe sisters were the only ways into the daily recognition that I am a well-loved daughter of God.

Walking in the practice of confession—both to God and to the safe community of believers—takes an intentional commitment. But this is what it means to walk in the light. And only in the light are the shameful secrets of our lives exposed; only there do we come face-to-face with the truth. John, the beloved disciple, stated it this way: "God is light, and there is no darkness in him at all. So we are lying if we say we have fellowship with God but go on living in spiritual darkness; we are not practicing the truth. But if we are living in the light, as God is in the light, then we have fellowship with each other, and the blood of Jesus, his Son, cleanses us from all sin" (1 John 1:5–7).

This letter from John is soaked in the love of God. The same John who walked along the shores of Galilee, who leaned his head on Jesus' breast, who refused to leave the brutal crucifixion site, and who saw the risen Christ is writing to us so beautifully about how we might have fellowship with God. And this fellowship implies a kindred love.

The ESV translation of verse 5 says, "This is the message we have heard from him and proclaim to you, that God is light, and in him is no darkness at all."

The word *message* he used at the beginning of this verse is only used twice in the New Testament. It's the Greek word *angelia*. It's related to the word *euangelion*, meaning life-giving gospel. The message of Christ—the good news—is not to be used to bruise and condemn but to give life. Real, lived-out-loud life.

The Aramaic translation of verse 5 reads like this: "This is the hope that we heard from him and give you hope because God is light and there is absolutely no darkness in him."

John heard Jesus talk about this hope, saw the Hope of hopes with his own eyes. John saw the darkest days of Christ's life—those days after His death—but he also saw how the light of God beat that darkness in Christ's resurrection. He knew that the hope and light of God our Father is limitless. The hope and light of God is all good news.

Perhaps one of your parents made you feel like a disappointment. You will never receive that soul-crushing message from God; His message is hope and light.

Maybe you were abused by someone close to you. Our God will never harm you; He is the Restorer of hope and light to the darkened, broken heart.

Perhaps your life has been peppered with disappointment—nothing life-altering, but still hard to bear. Or you compare yourself to other women and feel you don't quite measure up. You may have lost it with your children this morning, and now your heart condemns you. In those moments, He comes to you and says He is proud of you, His dearly loved daughter.

Whatever the baggage you've carried deep inside for so long, whatever darkness you've harbored, it's time to invite the hopeful light of God into it. And when you walk in His light, when nothing is hidden from Him, you'll find that God loves you just as you are, just where you are. The beauty of His grace means He won't leave you there.

Bringing your personal darkness into the light of God might be difficult at first, like coming out of a midday matinee into the brilliant sunshine. This kind of light can be blinding. But John makes it clear: We'll either follow Christ in the light, or we'll turn away and walk on in our own darkness. The invitation of the gospel is simple: *Come, walk with Me, and be fully known and fully loved.*

But John doesn't stop there. He goes on to say, "If we are living in the light, as God is in the light, then we have fellowship with each other" (v. 7). That's what makes it possible to have true fellowship: a community of people who are unafraid of bringing their pain, wounds, and secrets into God's light, a people who are unafraid of sharing their brokenness with each other. When we begin to grasp how much God loves us, even in our brokenness, we are able to love each other, to have true fellowship. And when we love each other this way, we can encourage each other to keep walking in the light of truth.

In the weeks and months following my mum's passing, I began to lean on the truth of God's Word in a deeper way. I began to reorder my thinking and to combat the darkness. Having a moment of pure joy in a restroom in Ayr, Scotland, was a gift, but I had to learn how to make that a daily practice. So, as I felt the darkness closing in, I chose a place to meet with God every day, to bring my darkness into the light. It wasn't something I added to my to-do list; it was simply my daily *who-I-am* place.

I began to sit on the little patio in our back garden, by the fountain where the water gushes from a lion's mouth. I began to meet my Father every day in a fresh, intimate way. I was at the beginning of a new adventure with God. I brought my Bible, a journal, a pen, a hymnbook, a large cup of coffee, and a worship playlist on my iPhone. And morning after morning, I brought the secret lies I believed into God's light. I listened as He reminded me that even in the darkness of my depression, I was well loved.

I still go to that chair in the morning. Some mornings I'll read from the hymnbook and let the words wash over me.

> *O Love that wilt not let me go,*
> *I rest my weary soul in thee;*
> *I give thee back the life I owe,*
> *That in thine ocean depths its flow*
> *May richer, fuller be.*

O light that followest all my way,
I yield my flickering torch to thee;
My heart restores its borrowed ray,
That in thy sunshine's blaze its day
May brighter, fairer be.

O Joy that seekest me through pain,
I cannot close my heart to thee;
I trace the rainbow through the rain,
And feel the promise is not vain,
That morn shall tearless be.[1]

I'll read through the Psalms, often making my way through Psalm 23. I find such companionship there. It's believed that Psalm 23 was the first one that David wrote when he was just a shepherd boy. Many mornings I'll read it as if he's my little brother sitting down on the grass beside me telling me what he's learned about our Father.

The LORD is my shepherd;
    I have all that I need.
He lets me rest in green meadows;
    he leads me beside peaceful streams.
    He renews my strength.
He guides me along right paths,
    bringing honor to his name.
Even when I walk
    through the darkest valley,
I will not be afraid,
    for you are close beside me.
Your rod and your staff
    protect and comfort me.
You prepare a feast for me
    in the presence of my enemies.

You honor me by anointing my head with oil.
My cup overflows with blessings.
Surely your goodness and unfailing love will pursue me
all the days of my life,
and I will live in the house of the LORD
forever.

Before he ever faced Goliath or King Saul, David made a daily practice of singing his heart out to God with only the sheep and goats for company. He could never have known what a friend he would be to you and me, what an example he'd set. I sing along with him many mornings. I make up my own tunes, as I can't quite hear his harp; but I do hear his heart and I join in.

The beauty of these daily practices of confession and meditation is that it's not about us getting them right. The practices are more about becoming fully known by our Father.

I wonder how much of your story is wrapped up tightly inside of you. The trouble with secrets and lies is that they're very believable when they're in the dark. When they're brought into the light of God and then into the light of the community of believers, they lose their power. And perhaps this is because you cannot understand grace in the dark. Grace lives in the light; it pours out into those who think they are broken beyond repair. It pours out into us, showing us how much God loves us, how much He wants to have fellowship with us.

Seeing ourselves loved changes how we see one another. As Philip Yancey wrote: "One who has been touched by grace will no longer look on those who stray as 'those evil people' or 'those poor people who need our help.' Nor must we search for signs of 'love-worthiness.' Grace teaches us that God loves because of who God is, not because of who we are."[2] This is why learning to live in the light brings us closer in fellowship with the people of the light, with our safe-place sisters.

Being loved by God and being loved and known in community

gives us the grace to reach out to those around us who are hurting, to those who feel as if they are dying on the inside a little more every day. We have been given life-changing truth, not only for ourselves but for serving a broken world. Living out this truth, you might be surprised at the secrets you allow those around you to unlock when you dare to show up with open hands and a transparent heart. You might be surprised how much you offer others when you bring all your secrets and shame into God's light, into the light of His community.

We have been given life-changing truth, not only for ourselves but for serving a broken world.

I'm grateful for my story now. I wouldn't have written it like this if I could have chosen, but it's brought me to the place I am today—loved and known. That's what I want for you. And as long as I have breath left in my body, I purpose to live out this calling until I see Jesus face-to-face: "But my life is worth nothing to me unless I use it for finishing the work assigned me by the Lord Jesus—the work of telling others the Good News about the wonderful grace of God" (Acts 20:24).

Reflection

I have a gratitude journal. Each day I intentionally look for things to be thankful for. Every morning when I wake up, that's a gift. So is a smile from a store clerk, a dog with a waggy tail, or a shoulder rub from my husband when I know he's tired too.

I invite you to join me in this practice. It might feel a little contrived at first, but something happens in us when we take our eyes off what's not working and give thanks for what is. Every time you feel yourself getting frustrated, stop. Find one thing to thank God for.

We're encouraged over and over in Scripture to develop a grateful heart. Here are a few verses to meditate on. Consider their different meanings about gratitude and pray for them to be true in your life. Then ask yourself: "What am I grateful for today?"

> This is the day that the LORD has made;
> let us rejoice and be glad in it.
>
> —Psalm 118:24 ESV

> Give thanks in all circumstances; for this is
>   the will of God in Christ Jesus for you.
>
> —1 Thessalonians 5:18 ESV

> Give thanks to the LORD, for he is good,
> for his steadfast love endures forever.
>
> —Psalm 136:1 ESV

> Since we are receiving a Kingdom that is
>   unshakable, let us be thankful and please God
>   by worshiping him with holy fear and awe.
>
> —Hebrews 12:28

> Giving thanks always and for everything to God the
>   Father in the name of our Lord Jesus Christ.
>
> —Ephesians 5:20 ESV

Chapter 12

❧

Miracles in the Middle of the Mess

A scar is what happens when the word is made flesh.

—LEONARD COHEN, *THE FAVOURITE GAME*

There was nothing unusual about the way that day began. It was a Thursday and I was doing what I've done at least a thousand Thursdays before: getting into my car to drive to the airport. My luggage was in the trunk, briefcase and jacket in the backseat, and coffee in my to-go mug. I opened the garage door, started the engine, and was about to put the car into reverse when I stopped. I sat for a moment wondering why I felt compelled to stop.

Had I forgotten something?

No. That wasn't it.

Did I remember to lock the back door?

That wasn't it either.

That's when it hit me. I was on the edge of a holy moment. The voice of God was speaking in my spirit.

I didn't hear an audible voice, but I felt the strong awareness that somewhere inside, the still, small voice of God was whispering. I stepped out of the car and stood quietly by the driver's side door, trying to listen to that small interior whisper. As I waited in the quiet, hands raised in expectation, I sensed that I was being given a new assignment.

As I've shared over the previous twenty years, I have lived under that mandate of Paul's commitment to the believers in Thessalonica: "We loved you so much that we shared with you not only God's Good News but our own lives, too" (1 Thess. 2:8). When I spoke, I brought together the power of the Word of God and the mercy of how God has met me in my brokenness. But as I stood in the garage, I wondered if that was changing. Was it time to put my story behind me?

But even as I asked God if that was what He wanted, I sensed that wasn't it. And in that moment, I had the strangest yet overwhelming desire to stand up taller. I'm only five feet four inches tall, so that's a tough call; but as I straightened as best I could, I felt as if I was coming to attention, as if I was receiving military orders. I sensed I was being called to fight in a new way. I wasn't sure at the time what it all meant, but I heard myself say, "Yes, Lord!" out loud. I stood in the garage for a few moments, hands raised, embracing whatever God willed.

The moment passed, so I got back into the car, started the engine, and drove to the airport. I boarded the airplane for a speaking engagement at a large women's conference in Springfield, Missouri, hosted by James River Church. I'd been a guest of Pastor John Lindell and his wife, Debbie, before, and I'd heard through mutual friends that God was moving Debbie into a new season of ministry after her brutal battle with breast cancer. I was anxious to be with her. Even more, I was anxious to see what God might do.

I smiled as I was escorted into the backstage greenroom at the arena that night. It was decorated to the hilt. There were plates of cookies with BELIEVE, the theme of the conference, piped in pink and white frosting. Pink and white roses were artistically arranged on each little table, and the chatter that often precedes the first night of a conference filled the room. There were three of us speaking that weekend—Debbie, Darlene Zschech, and me. We didn't connect before the event to compare notes, but God was about to weave a powerful message through all three of us. The power of Christ was about to shine through our wounds.

First Debbie spoke. She shared her battle scars—what it's like to journey through the darkness when cancer invades. What used to be the wide, well-lit path of life suddenly becomes a frightening, dark tunnel, Debbie said. Life becomes about one thing—battling the dragon that has invaded your body. She held nothing back, making it clear that it had been a rough fight, but there was strength in every word she spoke. Rather than diminishing her strength, Debbie's personal battle with cancer had fine-tuned it. As I watched her onstage that night, I saw the beauty that is born when brokenness is placed in the hands of a master Creator.

Debbie's courage, her ability to speak openly about her battle, took the disease that disfigures a woman's body and so often bruises her soul, and removed its power. She named the fear that always lurks in the shadows of any diagnosis, especially a cancer diagnosis; but as she shared, it became clear that her story wasn't simply one of survival. It was bigger than that.

She walked us through her tunnel of fear and helped us see that Christ had walked with her, even in her hardest moments. She didn't pretend that the journey was easy, but she'd made it through by the power of Christ, and there she was, standing in front of us, calling us out of our scary places together. She reminded us that what we believe about our lives affects everything.

If we believe we are loved, we will live loved.
If we believe we are strong in the power of God, we will live strong.
If we believe Christ is with us in our fear, we will be brave.
If we believe that Christ is with us in the mornings of life, He will be there at midnight too.

Darlene spoke next. I knew her as a powerful worship leader. Her song "Shout to the Lord" is a classic in many churches around the world. I'd witnessed her anointing to lead us into the presence of God in worship, but I'd never heard her speak before. It was powerful. She read this passage from the book of Isaiah:

> He gives power to the faint,
>> and to him who has no might he increases strength.
> Even youths shall faint and be weary,
>> and young men shall fall exhausted;
> but they who wait for the LORD shall renew their strength;
>> they shall mount up with wings like eagles;
> they shall run and not be weary;
>> they shall walk and not faint. (40:29–31 ESV)

I've heard many great messages on that text, but there was a quiet, confident beauty in the way Darlene spoke about what it means to wait for the Lord. She stood onstage, arms folded, tapping her foot—*waiting* the way so many of us often do. Her body language spoke volumes—*Come on, God, hurry up.*

Proper waiting, she said, was different. She stood quietly, leaning forward in anticipation. She was still, expectant. It was such a beautiful picture of a well-loved daughter waiting for the next word from her Father. It would have been a compelling enough picture if she'd learned it on the beaches of her homeland of Australia, but she'd learned it in the dark night of battle too.

As she spoke about her own journey with cancer, that passage of Scripture became flesh and blood before our eyes. She spoke of the days when every bit of strength was gone and all she could do was wait and lean on Christ. But where was He amid the pain and the fear?

Darlene shared of her exhaustion on one particular day when the effects of chemotherapy and the sickness in her body and soul were overwhelming. Her phone was lying beside her bed, and hearing the familiar ping of an incoming text message, she picked it up. It was from Debbie Lindell. They had never been in regular contact before, but Debbie felt compelled to reach out to this sister, thousands of miles away in Australia, and tell her, "I understand. You will get through this."

It was the reminder that Darlene needed: to know she was not alone. And this message was the pure, life-affirming gift of hope. Debbie had offered community, had become the broken bread and wine poured out for Darlene. Debbie had become the body of Christ in action, calling Darlene out of the lie that she wasn't going to make it and speaking life into the abject despair that fear can bring.

Debbie offered a small gesture in Darlene's season of darkness. And this gesture became such a lovely picture for the five thousand women in the arena. Darlene and Debbie showed what it looks like to be a safe place for each other, to confront lies, fear, and shame, and to dispel secrets. The comfort Darlene experienced from Christ was profound, yet God put it on the heart of another woman to speak into the hardest moments. Do you see the beauty and grace of that? God could have said, "I'm all you need." Instead, at her lowest moment, He sent a friend to say, "I'm here for you too." Christ comes to us in the safety of sisterhood, in the safety of community. Darlene made that clear.

As Darlene brought her message to a close, she invited the women in the arena who were in their own cancer battles to stand, and she prayed over them. It was powerful. The strength in Christ that Debbie had passed to Darlene now made its way around an arena full of women. Tears were shed and hope filled the room. It wasn't a traditional "healing" service—certainly not in the way I've understood it before. It was bigger than that. There was a recognition that some of the women in that arena might lose their cancer battles, but even still, a more significant battle was being won. It was the battle against fear, loneliness, and the shameful lies we tell ourselves. In the coming together as sisters it becomes clear: Our wounds were never meant for us alone.

I was scheduled to speak the following day, and as I woke that next morning and looked through my notes, I wondered if I should change my message. I wasn't sure if my encounter with God in the garage demanded a new direction, so I spread my notes and my Bible out on the bed and got down on my knees and prayed.

Here I am, Lord. Everything that's brought me to this place at this time I offer up to You. I'm holding nothing back. Do with me and through me as You will. Thank You for the honor of bearing Your name. Thank You for the scars that have brought me closer to You.

I was thirty minutes into a forty-minute message when I recognized that I should shift the conclusion. I'd planned on inviting women to respond to God and come to the altar, but what I sensed now was not the sort of altar call I'd ever given or experienced before. I paused for a moment, convinced that God was asking me to push into this new direction. So I asked the audience the unthinkable question: Is there anyone in the crowd who has ever attempted suicide or been plagued by suicidal thoughts like I'd been?

Then I asked, "If you're like me, would you be willing to join me at the front?"

I will never forget the next few moments. Women began to leave their seats and pour down to the front of the stage. They came from the back of the arena and from the balconies. I stood with tears pouring down my face as I looked at them. Some were in their teens and some were in their seventies. There were hundreds of them. I thought back to nights when I'd believed I was the only Christian in the world who struggled with suicidal thoughts. But as the women poured down the aisles, I saw how many there were. Some women had struggled with suicidal thoughts for most of their lives, and some for only a short while. But here they were, and the thought struck me: we were not alone.

Something rose up in me on that stage, and I swear my five-foot-four stature stretched to six feet. I felt fierce, confident. I looked at the women who remained in their seats, the community of women who didn't struggle with suicide or depression, and I asked each to stretch out her hands toward the struggling daughters of God as a sign that we were standing together. Then, I prayed.

I asked God to shine His light into our darkness.

I asked Him to breathe hope into the stagnant filth of despair.

I asked for His truth to penetrate the lies we had all believed for so long.

Then I closed with a scripture I have loved since I was a child:

> The LORD is my light and my salvation;
>> whom shall I fear?
> The LORD is the stronghold of my life;
>> of whom shall I be afraid? (Ps. 27:1 ESV)

I have shared the first verse of Psalm 27 hundreds of times in my life. But that night, for the very first time, I declared the final two verses of Psalm 27 out loud over each one of us who chose to stand in the light. And that night I believed these words:

> I believe that I shall look upon the goodness of the LORD
>> in the land of the living!
> Wait for the LORD;
>> be strong, and let your heart take courage;
>> wait for the LORD! (27:13–14 ESV).

As I spoke, something became crystal clear. When we try to hide our wounds, our scars, our cancers, all those things we believe make us less lovely, we make fear and shame the stronghold of our lives.

When we bring our

wounds to Christ,

when we out our

secrets and shame,

we make Him the

stronghold of our lives,

and He uses our wounds

for His *purposes.*

But when we bring our wounds to Christ, when we out our secrets and shame, we make Him the stronghold of our lives, and He uses our wounds for His purposes. He makes something beautiful of us.

It's the antithesis of what we feel must be true. Can you imagine what the church would be like if we all told the truth with gentleness and courage? It's not that we want to become the poster children for depression or cancer or disappointment or struggle; we just want to put those things in their place. Yes, bad things happen, but we are not alone. Jesus prepared us.

If you've experienced a suicide among your family or friends, then you probably know that a common thought about suicide is that it is an act of cowardice. That *can* be true. If someone has created financial or relational chaos in their lives and it's about to be exposed, suicide may seem like an easy way out. But to those who have struggled with mental illness, suicide is slipping over the edge. For those weary warriors, suicide is not an easy way out; it's the only thing left that makes sense to them in that moment. The dark night of mental illness is suffocating. In that kind of despair, it's hard to reason. You just want the pain to stop.

I attended the funeral of a young married man who took his life after a long battle with crippling depression. It was a sad occasion. After the service, many of us joined the family for coffee. While the young widow was out of the room, a couple of people made the remark that this was the act of a coward.

With tears pouring down my face, I said, "All you see is that he ended his life at twenty-six. What you've missed is how bravely he fought for twenty-six years, and that he said yes to life and to Christ." I don't pretend to understand what takes place in those final moments between a broken believer and God's suffering servant, the risen Christ, but I do believe this: when desperate children of God take their own lives, God may not have called them home, but He welcomes them home.

I shared the story of my dad's suicide at a little church in New

England last year. I talked about the assurance I have that my dad is safely home with Christ. At the end of the service two women brought a young girl to me. She must have been about sixteen, with long dark hair, pale skin, and sunken eyes. She was crying so hard she could hardly stand, so we sat together on the steps leading up to the platform. Finally, she told me about her father's long battle with mental illness. She said that he was an amazing dad who loved Jesus and his family well, but one night he took his life. Her next words were heartbreaking. "I was told that my dad is in hell because he took his life."

What cruelty in the name of Christianity! Suicide may be a sin, but it is not the unpardonable sin. The only unforgivable sin is to reject Christ. Remember this glorious assurance from Paul: "And I am convinced that nothing can ever separate us from God's love. Neither death nor life, neither angels nor demons, neither our fears for today nor our worries about tomorrow—not even the powers of hell can separate us from God's love" (Rom. 8:38).

Nothing, nothing, nothing can ever separate us from God's love.

Nothing, nothing, nothing can ever
separate us from God's love.

If you're like me and you struggle with suicidal thoughts, or if you self-harm in any way, I invite you to join me in a prayer. Copy this onto a card or take a screenshot with your phone so that you have this at hand when the darkness strikes. *Because you are not alone.* When the darkness hits, you may feel alone, abandoned, and afraid. I know what despair tastes like, and I know the lie that says it would be better for everyone if you were no longer here. It sounds true, but it comes from the pit of hell. We stand together and declare in Jesus' name that we will live to see the goodness of the Lord in the land of the living.

> Lord Jesus Christ,
>> I am broken but You died so that I might find healing.
>> You were rejected so that I could be fully accepted.
>> I choose life now in Your powerful name.
>> I am Your well-loved child on the days when I feel it and on the days when I don't.
>> I refuse to listen to the lies of the enemy anymore, and I confess with my mouth that in Jesus' name, I will live!
>> Amen.

Amen, my friend.

We've not been promised a life of ease. Instead, Jesus assured us of something very different. In the gospel of John, Jesus says, "I have told you all this so that you may have peace in me. Here on earth you will have many trials and sorrows. But take heart, because I have overcome the world" (16:33).

The "all this" that Jesus is speaking about are the trials and tribulations the disciples would experience. In the preceding chapters of John, Jesus told the disciples that persecution was coming, and in fact, there would come a time when those who persecuted and executed them would think they were doing it for God. Even still, He assured them that they could have peace in the darkness of the world because He'd overcome it. In a few sentences, Christ de-mythicized what it meant to follow Him on this earth. Things would be hard and confusing, but the ultimate battle had already been won. And Jesus walked this same road as He endured His own suffering for the sake of the world.

Every note in Christ's story is a melody we're invited to join. His wounds became scars that purchased our healing. Recall these words from the prophet Isaiah:

Surely he took up our pain
and bore our suffering,
yet we considered him punished by God,
stricken by him, and afflicted.
But he was pierced for our transgressions,
he was crushed for our iniquities;
the punishment that brought us peace was on him,
and by his wounds we are healed. (53:4–5 NIV)

The truth of Isaiah 53 is layered. This much is clear, though: Christ took on the punishment for all the sin of the world so that when you and I receive Him, we have peace with God. The wounds He bore healed the chasm that existed between us and a holy God. But I believe that there's more. He suffered in every way that we suffer. Death, life, betrayal, abandonment, and excruciating pain. Jesus didn't hide the hard bits from us, so we get to see it all. That's not by accident. He shared His story and His agony with us, His family of faith. And when we share how His story has brought us life, we bear witness to a world that so desperately needs healing.

As a follower of Jesus, there is power in your story when you don't hide it. Your authority lies in your scars. I can't speak to things I've never struggled with; I can only confess my story, invite Christ into it, then invite you into it too. And you can do the same.

Our stories are different. Perhaps you're struggling with the disappointment of a marriage that's not all you hoped and dreamed it would be.

Maybe you struggle with someone at work or church or in your family. Perhaps it's your mother-in-law. Maybe it feels as if someone has ruined your perfect place.

Maybe you just don't like living in your own skin. You compare yourself to other women, and as far as you're concerned, you don't measure up.

It could be your children. Perhaps you've prayed for children, and month after month your prayers seem to bounce back off the ceiling.

When you lose your health it's hard not to lose your hope. Getting older presents its own challenges when you can't do the things you once could.

No matter your circumstances, here's the truth: You have a story, and that story has its own peculiar mess. You can confess that story to Christ and let go. You can let Him start a work of healing, even now, right in the middle of your mess. You can also confess your story to your sisters; you can let them know they are not alone. The truth is, I need to hear your story, and other women need to hear your story. In the sacrament of sharing we feel less alone, and we create safe spaces for others to say "me too." Our example makes it safe for them to bring their stories of pain to Christ for healing. In the sacrament of sharing, we also come to understand how loved and accepted we are by Christ, and by the safe sisters God has provided for us. Together we find strength for this beautiful, broken life.

In bringing our shame and fear to the stronghold of the Lord, we mimic the path of Jesus. And just like Jesus, as we overcome our shame and fear, as Christ works resurrection in our lives, we become beacons of hope. Don't you want to live this kind of life?

This, I suppose, is my closing prayer. I hope to live a life so open to Christ that He knows my every secret and shame. I hope, too, that I become like the Samaritan woman at the well in John 4, who went into the world and declared to her townspeople, "Come and see a man who told me everything I ever did!" (v. 29).

Though her brokenness was completely known by Jesus, she felt His complete love and acceptance. And that love and acceptance encouraged her to build a bridge for others to find Christ. That's not just her story; it's ours as well. When we bring our secret shame to Christ for healing, when we experience His love and acceptance, we want nothing more than to bring others into this same experience.

And when the world sees person after person stepping into the healing presence of Christ, they want to follow suit.

This kind of confessional living is not a Sunday-morning or Wednesday-night thing. It's a 24/7, right-in-the-middle-of-your-mess kind of calling. It's a calling to let people know this glorious, riotous message:

> The people walking in darkness
>   have seen a great light;
>   on those living in the land of deep darkness
>   a light has dawned. (Isa. 9:2 NIV)

I believe one of the greatest miracles of all is that when we live this open, transparent, beautifully broken life, we find true strength in finally understanding who we have always been: well-loved daughters of our Father God.

Reflection

When Christian was a little boy and he was finally tucked up in bed at night after prayers and stories, I would walk to the bedroom door, stop, turn, and ask him this question: "Which boy does Mommy love?" He would put his little hand on his chubby cheek and with a big grin say, "This boy."

He said it with absolute conviction because he knew it was true. He was and is a well-loved boy.

That's what I want for you. I have prayed and wept over this book. I so want you to know in the deepest part of who you are that you are never called to be perfect. Rather, you are perfectly loved.

In 2017 we celebrate the five hundredth anniversary of Martin Luther posting his "Ninety-Five Theses" on the church door in

Wittenberg, Germany. This was the beginning of the Protestant Reformation. For years believers had struggled to keep the law, to get it all right. Luther himself was known to spend hour after hour trying to think up any little forgotten sin, but no matter how often he confessed, he found no comfort. One day as he was studying the book of Romans he had what he called a lightning bolt of inspiration. Luther's revolutionary message was that sinners are justified by grace through faith, not by getting everything right. The message of grace transformed him. It should. It's the best news of all.

You are loved.
You are accepted.
You are invited to be your real, authentic, quirky self.

That kind of love changes how we see the mess. The mess is temporary, but the love will get us all the way home.

I have one final request. Each time you catch your reflection in a mirror, a store window, or even a puddle, would you ask yourself this question?

"Which girl does Jesus love?"

Then put your hand on your lovely cheek and say with confidence, "This girl."

That's the scarlet ribbon that runs through this book. God's love is hope and life. It's confession and prayer and silence and gratitude. It's telling the truth and exposing the secrets. It's being known and coming into community. It's life! It's saying out loud, "I am not alone. I am loved, and I am strong."

Acknowledgments

I am profoundly grateful to the following people for their invaluable help in writing this book.

Seth Haines, you are much more than a gifted editor. You are a raw, real, brave, tell-the-whole-truth fellow warrior. You shared more than your gift with Barry and me, you shared your life and left an indelible mark on our hearts, little brother of mine.

Jenny Baumgartner, I am so aware of how you shaped this book for good from beginning to end. You saw the big picture when I would get bogged down in the details. I left every conversation feeling like I had been given a gift. Thank you.

Jeff James, Stephanie Tresner, and Sara Broun, thank you for your patience when I got so picky with every little word that expressed the heart of this book. I am so grateful for your enthusiasm and commitment to spread this message of hope. You are gifts of grace.

Janene MacIvor, you feel like family to me. You have lovingly shepherded so many of my books, gently reminded me of deadlines and cheered me on every step of the way. Thank you.

Thank you to Milkglass Creative for patiently presenting so many versions of cover art until I knew it was the right one. I love your work.

To Brian Hampton and the whole team at Nelson Books a huge thank you for many miles traveled together and lives impacted for the kingdom of Christ.

To my husband, Barry, and son, Christian, you above all others know what it's like to love someone who struggles with the dark night of depression. You make me smile when I feel sad. You hold me when I feel like I'm falling. We share an understand of commitment that goes far beyond what makes us feel good to what makes us more like Jesus to a broken world. I love you both so much.

Jesus Christ, Son of God, my Savior and Lord, you are my hope, my life, the light in my darkest corners. Thank you for putting on human flesh to walk where we walk, to understand where we struggle, to die for us and rise again. Your resurrection changes everything. Because you live—we live.

Notes

Chapter 1: Everyday Salvation

1. Frederick Buechner, *Telling the Truth: The Gospel as Tragedy, Comedy, and Fairy Tale* (New York: HarperCollins, 1997), 23.
2. Nicky Gumbel, "The Three Tenses of Salvation," Bible in One Year, September 14 reading, https://www.bibleinoneyear.org/bioy /commentary/1005.

Chapter 3: The Walls We Build

1. For more on Project Semicolon, visit their website: http://www .projectsemicolon.org.

Chapter 4: You Don't Have to Hide

1. Frederick Buechner, *Beyond Words: Daily Readings in the ABC's of Faith* (New York: HarperCollins, 2004), 65.

Chapter 6: Let Go

1. Ziya Meral, "Bearing the Silence of God," *Christianity Today*, March 19, 2008, http://www.christianitytoday.com/ct/2008/march /29.41.html.

Chapter 7: Beautifully Broken

1. A. W. Tozer, *The Pursuit of God* (Dallas: Gold House Books, 2017).

Chapter 8: Rejecting the Lies We've Believed

1. Dietrich Bonhoeffer, *Life Together* (New York: Harper & Row, 1954), 116.

Chapter 9: Get Back Up

1. Charles Spurgeon, "Songs in the Night," *The Complete Works of C. H. Spurgeon*, vol. 44 (Harrington, DE: Delmarva, 2013).
2. Charles Spurgeon, "Job's Resignation," *The Complete Works of C. H. Spurgeon*, vol. 42 (Harrington, DE: Delmarva, 2013).
3. Franz J. Leenhardt, quoted in Leon Morris, *The Epistle to the Romans* (Grand Rapids: Wm. B. Eerdmans, 1988), 435.

Chapter 10: You Are Braver Than You Know

1. J. C. Ryle, *Expository Thoughts on the Gospels, St. John*, vol. 3 (London: William Hunt & Co., n.d.), 332. Ryle is commenting on John 19:17.

Chapter 11: Fully Known and Fully Loved

1. George Matheson, "O Love That Wilt Not Let Me Go," 1882.
2. Philip Yancey, *What's So Amazing About Grace?* (Grand Rapids: Zondervan, 2003), 89.

About the Author

❦

Sheila Walsh is a Scottish lass known as "the encourager" to the more than 5.5 million women she's met and spoken to around the world. She loves being a Bible teacher, making God's Word practical, and sharing her own story of how God met her when she was at her lowest point and lifted her up again.

Sheila also enjoys being an author—in fact, she likes to write every day—and has sold more than 5 million books. She is the cohost of the television program *Life Today* with James and Betty Robison, airing in the United States, Canada, Europe, and Australia.

Calling Texas home, Sheila lives in Dallas with her husband, Barry; her son, Christian; and three little dogs—Belle, Tink, and Maggie.

You can stay in touch at

sheilawalsh.com

facebook.com/sheilawalshconnects

Instagram @sheilawalsh1

Also available from

Sheila Walsh

In this six-session video Bible study, Sheila Walsh enters a new arena of equipping women with a practical method for connecting with God's strength and leaning on it in the midst of struggle.

For more information, visit
InTheMiddleOfTheMessBook.com